SCENIC
SOUTH AFRICA

AUGUST SYCHOLT
PETER SCHIRMER

Struik Publishers (Pty) Ltd
(a member of The Struik Publishing Group (Pty) Ltd)
Cornelis Struik House
80 McKenzie Street
Cape Town 8001

Reg. No.: 54/00965/07

First published as *This is South Africa* in 1981
First published in softcover in 1985
Second impression 1988
Third impression 1989
Fourth impression 1990
Fifth impression 1992
First published as *Scenic South Africa* in 1994
Second edition 1996

Editor (1994 edition): Brenda Brickman
Editor (1996 edition): Joy Clack
Cover design: Lyndall Hamilton
Designer: Neville Poulter
Map: John Loubser
Typesetter: Richard Williams

Photoset by Unifoto (Pty) Ltd, Cape Town
Reproduction by cymk prepress
Printing and binding by Kyodo Printing Co. (Pte) Ltd, Singapore

ISBN 1 86825 934 X

The graceful proportions of a gabled Cape Dutch homestead
(frontispiece) are an ever-present link between the history of
the western Cape and its agricultural present – a gentle scene in
striking contrast to the stark majesty of the Drakensberg (title
page). Both, though, are as integral a part of South Africa as a
young Xhosa initiate (**3**) or a thundering lorry traversing the
landscape near Newcastle (**4**) where ox-wagons once rolled
across the veld.

SCENIC
SOUTH AFRICA

His stumpy legs were so short and weak that they could move
his grotesque body only when the mud and ooze of the
primeval swamp helped bear his mass. His tremendously thick
cranium contained a minute brain, and though scientists were
to call him a 'fearsome head', he was an inoffensive herbivore
who existed on a diet of ferns and cycads. He was
Tapinocephalus, and approximately 200 million years ago he
lurched through the vast, steaming swamps of Gondwanaland
where today the semi-desert of South Africa's Karoo bakes
aridly in the sun.

Save as fossils, nothing of his world remains except the
cycads, which still flourish in several parts of the Republic
and are unique to her flora. The swamp he inhabited was
compressed and changed as ice ages came and receded.
Tremendous geomorphic forces deep within the earth's core
rent Gondwanaland to form, among others, South America,
South Africa and Australasia. And these same forces spewed
forth the volcanic pipes which were to give the Republic her
diamond riches, while others laid down a vast sedimentary
saucer of gold whose rim is mined today to provide the
backbone of South Africa's economy.

Tapinocephalus is remembered only by scientists, and his
ancient presence commemorated by a reconstruction in the
South African Museum in Cape Town. But, as one of the first
mammal-like reptiles, he was an important link in the
evolutionary chain which was to provide the subcontinent
with the unsurpassed range of animal life found here today.
And though the vast herds of game that once teemed across the
country no longer exist – scattered and compressed by the

△**3**

advent of man – their descendants are to be seen, occasionally in the few wild spaces that remain but more frequently in the country's numerous game parks and reserves which are dedicated to their preservation.

Their predecessors never knew the safety of such sanctuaries. Excavations have revealed that the early man-apes – found at Taung and 900 000 years older than Neanderthal man – were effective prototypes for Man the Predator. Scientists have also discovered that the Stone-Age peoples who inhabited much of the subcontinent 25 000 years ago possessed relatively refined hunting techniques. Their hunter-gatherer existence was, in fact, little different to that of the San who for millennia shared the 1 134 100 km² that is South Africa with fauna which they killed for food or in self-defence. Pockets of these little people, whose social structure is based on sharing, still exist. But rock paintings in the shelters and caves they inhabited show that once they roamed the whole wide land from the sparkling coastal beaches to the rugged inland ranges and from the lush subtropical forest of the east to the timeless deserts of the west, where the remnants of their people still maintain something of their ancient life style.

They knew of the underground honeycomb that is the Cango Caves, but lacked powerful light to explore the natural gallery of its stalactites and stalagmites which spotlights now reveal – a wonderland for today's visitor. Some of these early San may have paused beside a sapling yellowwood in the Knysna Forest, never imagining that 1 700 years later the modern tourist would crane his or her neck in an attempt to see its tip towering 42 m above the ground, or marvel as he or she paced its 8-m girth. Certainly they themselves marvelled at the force of the Orange River as it thundered over its series of cascades, for they gave the Augrabies Falls its name 'the great waters', which the Korana tribes corrupted to auKarabis, and we, in turn, corrupted to its present form.

But the San were gradually driven from the land. Black tribes arrived from the north, moving ever south and westwards with the herds of cattle that were their wealth. Much later, white settlers – sent to the Cape to establish a victualling post for the ships of the Dutch East India Company en route to gather the riches of the Orient – expanded outwards to the north and east. Both were foreign to the land; both were to leave an indelible stamp on it – and continue to do so. Both were to multiply here, so that today about 43 million people inhabit the country – about eight times as many as at the turn of the century. The black African population stands at over 30 million, the white at around 5 million (compared with the less than 100 that comprised the first colonial settlement) and the Afro-European and Indian at over 4 million. The population as a whole is expanding at a rapid, even alarming rate.

The meeting of black and white and the clash of their disparate cultures was traumatic, leading to bloodshed which was to continue for centuries. But confrontation was not new to this part of Africa. From ancient times intertribal conflict was part and parcel of traditional tribal life. It heightened during Shaka's forging of the Zulu nation and the *Mfecane,* or period of forced migrations, which followed.

And it was the white colonists' need to expand that led to the protracted series of Frontier Wars, spanning more than a century, in which first the Dutch and then the British were to clash with the Xhosa tribes. These people, never defeated in battle, were brought down by the predictions of a young prophetess whose visions persuaded them to destroy their crops and to kill their cattle.

It was to act as a buffer between the established settlements of the Western Cape and the black tribes that the 1820 Settlers were brought from Britain – to leave a greater English imprint on the country than that of any colonial administration. And it was to escape the ongoing conflict and the rigidity of laws which stemmed from it that the Boer farmers were to venture inland on their 'Great Trek', opening up the hinterland for the eventual discovery of gold and diamonds, the first pointers to South Africa's vast mineral treasure-house.

These stubborn pioneers were the first to counter the might of the Zulu armies. Their epic journey and the greatest clash between black and white is commemorated in the Voortrekker Monument on a koppie outside Pretoria. Surrounded by an imitation bas-relief of 60 laagered ox-wagons in a protective circle around its base, it remains to many Afrikaners the most important tangible symbol of their nationhood. For them it is a symbol not only of physical but also spiritual significance. Through a specially placed aperture in the monument's roof, precisely at noon on December 16 each year, the rays of the sun strike through the vaulted ceiling to touch the centre of the cenotaph beneath – on the day most spiritually significant in the calendar of many Afrikaners. It was on this day in 1838

that a small but well-armed force of Trekkers met in bloody conflict, 100 years later that foundation stones of the monument were laid, and in 1949 it was officially opened.

But the land had not seen the last of bloodshed, for white was to clash with white in the pain and horror of two wars as the two small Boer republics withstood the might of the British Empire to defend their political beliefs, even as the shields and *assegais* of the Zulus had withstood the firepower of the whites to defend Zulu land and culture.

The uneasy truce that followed the Anglo-Boer War led to the creation of the modern South African state. But the clash of cultures persisted throughout the eight decades following Union, and it was only in 1994 that South Africa's leaders finally managed to fashion the blueprint for a wholly nonracial society – and in doing so set the country on a course to becoming a shining model for other troubled communities, both within and beyond the continent of Africa.

5△   7▽

Starkly etched skyscapers and the needle of the Post Office tower throw Johannesburg's skyline into sharp relief against the dying reds and golds of a highveld sunset (**5**). A mining camp scarcely a century ago, today the second largest city on the African continent retains a youthful brashness which the mature elements – the encircling freeways, futuristic high-rise buildings of glass and steel and other modern developments – cannot conceal.

The streets of central Johannesburg are long and narrow, for when gold was first found here the Transvaal Republican authorities reacted cautiously to the news, believing that the seam was a modest one, and that the mines would be short-lived. Johan Rissik, the Government Surveyor, set aside a waterless expanse of bushveld terrain and instructed the planners to lay out a town in close grid in order to create the maximum number of corner plots. These were considered

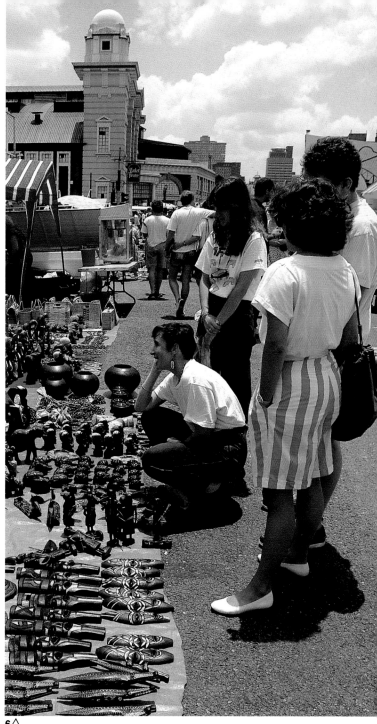

▽8   6△

more valuable and thus great spinners of revenue for the coffers of Paul Kruger's young republic. In the event, the first of them was sold on 10 December 1886 for half-a-crown, others for only 30 shillings, which was less than a barrel of drinking water fetched at the time.

Today Johannesburg is the country's premier city, a bustling cosmopolitan metropolis girded by dense rings of satellite towns huddling in an area known as the Witwatersrand and which, collectively, generates around half of South Africa's national income. Despite its youth and its rugged no-nonsense materialism, though, the place has real claims to sophistication, even stylishness.

The shopping malls rival the world's best; fine cuisine is offered by a myriad restaurants; the social scene is exuberant; the visual and performing arts thrive. Among the prominent venues is the Market Theatre (**8**), a four-auditorium complex that caters for tastes ranging from local and experimental drama to drawing-room comedy. The building, which once functioned as the Indian fruit and citrus market, also encloses a shopping arcade, art gallery, restaurant, bistro and jazz bar. The theatre fronts onto Fitzgerald Square, which hosts one of the city's bigger and most popular flea markets (**6**). Central Johannesburg does not offer a great deal of greenery – space is in short supply and nearly all of it has been filled by modern high-rise concrete and glass – but the surrounding suburbs are graced by some 600 carefully-tended parks and open spaces, among them charming Emmarentia Dam (**7**).

Where the streets of other early towns were planned to be wide enough for an ox-wagon and its team to turn in, those of central Johannesburg – lined on each side by parked vehicles – would make such a manoeuvre impossible, for even the smallest modern car. And, in the rush-hour, drivers may well envy the oxen's speed as traffic travels through the Hillbrow dusk (9), leaving the business centre almost deserted as the daily motorcades of commuters return to the suburbs. In Hillbrow's high-walled arteries the human pulse of the city beats for 24 hours of every day, and the strum of a street musician's guitar (10) is as likely to be heard at midnight as at noon.

11△ 12▽ 13▽

But it is for its vibrant business pulse that Johannesburg is internationally renowned. Its modern stock exchange – whose glass-sided lifts (12) provide a pigeon's-eye view of what was once the Ferreira's town camp (infant Johannesburg was divided into four separate areas, each of which is now an inner suburb) – has one of the busiest trading floors of any of the world's bourses. Though it was not the first stock exchange in South Africa – in the heyday of the De Kaap Valley diggings of Mpumalanga, just before the discovery of the Witwatersrand fields in 1886, the Barberton camp boasted two exchanges – it is the only one to have lasted, coming a long way from the early days when miners and speculators exchanged scrip 'between the chains' – literally old wagon chains strung from posts on a piece of dry, barren veld.

While still the 'City of Gold' in the world's imagination, or *Egoli* – literally 'gold' – to South Africa's 30 million blacks, in economic terms Johannesburg today is the centre of the Republic's industrial heartland – the Gauteng province, whose factories produce a kaleidoscopic range of products rivalled by the Aladdin's Cave of international wares available in the city's shops. In malls and arcades such as the rotunda beneath the Carlton Centre (11), Japanese transistor radios, leather goods from Italy, German cameras and *haute couture* Parisienne silks reveal the Johannesburger's materialistic progress, symbols of the hustler city's success. The towering 51-storey Carlton Centre is regarded with pride by most of *Egoli's* inhabitants as the true 'symbol of modern Johannesburg'. The complex is dominated by a 222-metre-tall tower block which is the world's largest reinforced concrete building as well as the tallest building in Africa. Modern Johannesburg is a far cry from the ragged tents and corrugated-iron shacks which spawned South Africa's biggest, busiest and most modern city.

14△ 15▽

The vast web of Soweto (**14**), the 'city within a city', is home to an estimated three million people. Every day from this urban sprawl which crouches on the south-western flank of Johannesburg, hundreds of thousands of people commute daily into *Egoli* and to the factories on Johannesburg's periphery. It was on the streets of Soweto that many of the battles against the evils of apartheid were waged and it was here that students led a protest march against Afrikaans instruction in their schools on the fateful day of 16 June 1976. The response to this protest resulted in the death of many people, including a young black pupil named Hector Petersen, and

16△ 17▽

the unleashing of pent-up fury and waves of destruction which followed spread across the land like wild fire. Eventually the fire was contained but the process of liberation that it started was unstoppable.

Soweto's little matchbox houses, the creation of faceless central planning, march in dull monotony across the dry and barren veld. Absolute uniformity is broken only by the arbitrary positioning of the homes on their respective sites. Overcrowding in these little houses is chronic and job opportunities in the township are virtually non-existent as Soweto was never meant to be anything besides a source of labour for the nearby city of Johannesburg. The schools are overflowing and yet the streets are filled with children who have never seen the inside of a classroom (15).

Nevertheless, Soweto is also a place of hope. Its children who do manage to find a place at school have a bubbling happiness and they carry with them the hope of a better world (17). In many ways Soweto is proof of the indomitable nature of man. Despite the rapacity of an ideology which required that Soweto's residents should be temporary sojourners – and therefore investment in socio-economic infrastructure and development should be kept to a minimum – and despite being victims of the cold bureaucracy that implemented this policy, the spirit of the people prevailed and a myriad entrepreneurs have set up small businesses. As a result of these initiatives Soweto now boasts a number of commercial centres and an expanding economic base.

The quality of life is being improved through the creation of stadia (16) and the development of sport, of which soccer is the uncrowned king. Among South African blacks, soccer is as much a cult as rugby is among whites. And it was in such soccer stadiums as those of Soweto that the very first multiracial sides were fielded – breaching the now-dismantled apartheid system and setting the lead for other athletic spheres.

◁ 18

19△   20▽

The rapid urbanisation of South Africa's rural and hitherto traditional people has created a society in transition with its own set of values and norms. Within the new social structures that have resulted, much of the new urban way of life has been absorbed within a traditional context (**19**). It is in the metaphysical world that the retention of traditional values and practices is strongest. Of great importance in this regard is the role of the *isangoma*, or diviner (**18, 20**), who has a special relationship with the ancestors and through this relationship is able to divine the cause of things going wrong. The *isangoma* may use various means of

divination, such as the throwing of bones or the use of divining rods, *izibulo*. Being mediums they are able to contact the ancestral spirits and prescribe medicines according to their dictates. These are obtained from the *inyanga* (herbalist) and are made from various ingredients such as plants, roots, bark and animal parts.

South Africa's highest ranking *sangoma* – known as a *sanusi* – is Credo Mutwa, who caused a furore among his peers when he published two books, *Indaba my Children* and *Africa is my Witness*, which purported to reveal the history of southern Africa's blacks and their medical and spiritual 'secrets'. Despite the scorn with which many greeted his revelations, Mutwa continues to enjoy a thriving practice.

The diviners' strength lies partly in the power of their medicines and partly in their ability to deal with the psyche of the patient. To many black patients the cause of their ailments are not due to the malfunctioning of some part of their body, but rather to the action of some extraneous force or from other people placing a curse or spell upon them. The power of the *isangoma* thus lies in his or her ability to deal with that force and lift the spell or curse.

The herbalists' strength lies in the power of their medicines. Some may be placebos, but modern research has found that many are pharmaceutically sound. Herbalist shops abound, not only in the townships but also downtown in many of South Africa's cities.

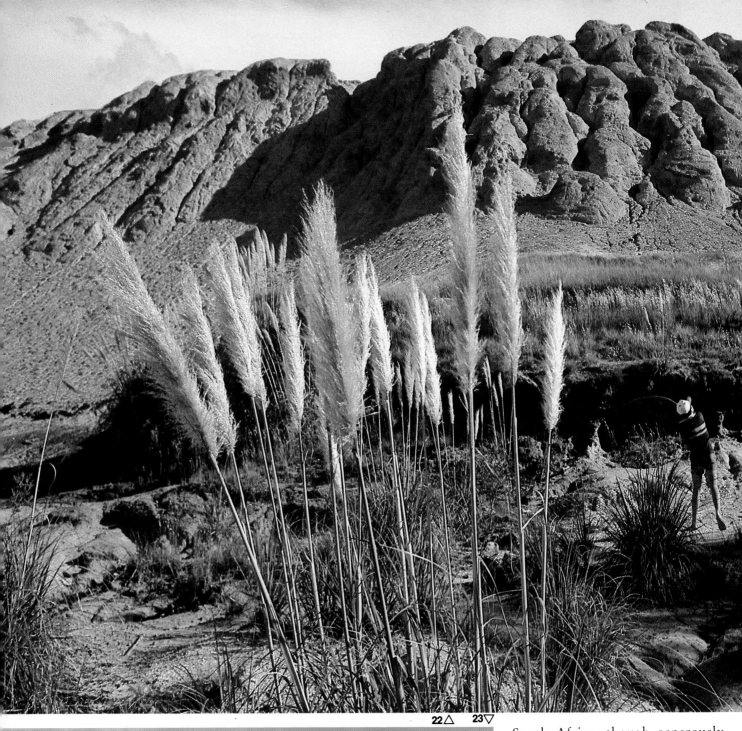

South Africa, though generously endowed with many other minerals, is synonymous with gold and the mine dumps – titanic refuse heaps of crushed reef from which the precious metal has been extracted – are a constant reminder of the Midas riches which lie beneath the Highveld landscape. From this region has come 40% of all the world's gold in the past century. The goldfields lie in a great 500-km arc from Evander in the north-east to Virginia in the south, on what geologists believe to be the rim of a giant gold saucer laid down approximately 2 700 million years ago and since covered by deposits of sedimentary and volcanic rock.

▷ 24

25 ▽

Even with today's sophisticated techniques, more than three tonnes of rock have to be crushed for every ounce of gold recovered, and the older dumps, such as this one at Maraisburg (**22**), bear silent testimony to the back-breaking efforts of the first miners. Something of the problems with which they had to contend, and their often primitive equipment, can be gleaned from this old steam locomotive (**24**), an active work-horse and a tourist attraction at one of Johannesburg's older mines.

The simplicity of the early methods of recovery, coupled with the rising price of gold, has provided a bonus for modern technology. Since 1978, residual gold has been recovered from the chemical recycling of old dumps and slime dams. But the bulk of the 550 tonnes of gold which South African mines produce each year, and which comprises just under a third of the world's output, is recovered far beneath the surface. From narrow stopes, often little more than a metre high, the ore-bearing rock and the miners are hauled upwards by special lifts, their presence marked by headgear like this (**23**) on an old mine south of Johannesburg. Once on the surface, the rock is washed, sorted and crushed before being ground into 'fines' which then undergoes a complex chemical process to extract the gold. It is then smelted and poured to form the 31,1 kg gold ingots containing 83% gold and 9% silver, which are further refined in Germiston. Even there these gold-green bricks don't reach absolute purity, but a fineness of 996 parts in 1 000. This special ingot (**25**) is on display at the Chamber of Mines in Johannesburg.

26△　27▽

▷
28

A molten stream of gold cascades into a mould (**26**) at West Driefontein, the world's richest mine, which has yielded nearly 2 000 000 kg of gold since operations first started in February 1952. A deep-level mine, from which more than 17 tonnes of water have to be pumped for every tonne of ore-bearing rock recovered, West Driefontein's workings plunge about two kilometres below the surface. At these depths, despite refrigerated air being pumped through the honeycomb of tunnels, temperatures of 32 °C are not uncommon, and humidity often reaches saturation.

Deeper into the earth's crust – at Western Deep Levels gold is being recovered 3,6 km underground – temperatures are correspondingly higher, reaching 60 °C at the actual work-face. This intense heat, combined with the unstable nature of the rock through which the stopes are driven, creates discomfort and hazards which continuing research attempts to alleviate. Sophisticated machinery has been

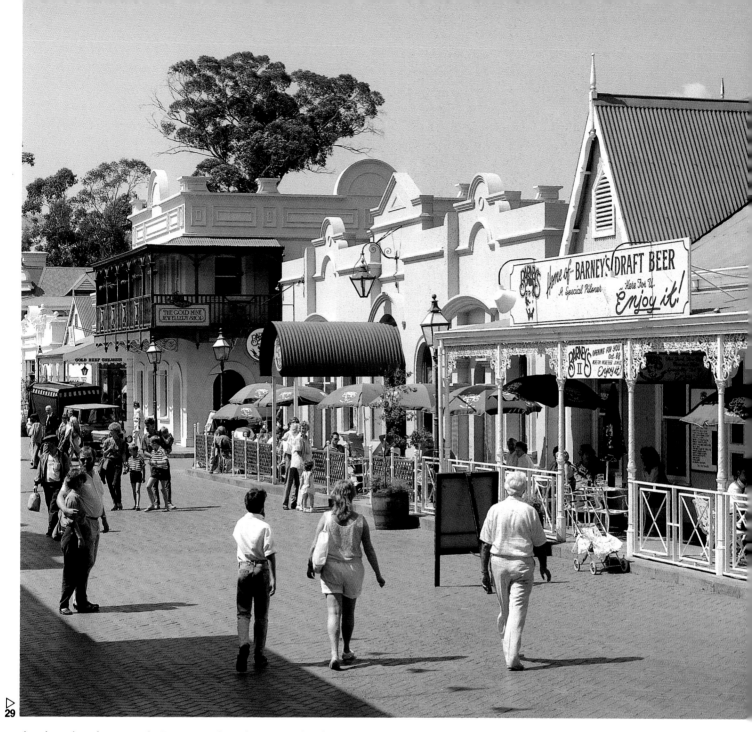

developed and new techniques employed as a result of this research process, but in the shallow stopes, working in Stygian darkness broken only by the comforting gleam of his headlamp (**27**), it is still the miner who must pit his strength against Nature's subterranean forces which can suddenly erupt, causing injury or death. But intensive safety precautions and elaborate techniques which warn of potential dangers have greatly reduced the risks of deep-level mining.

None of the 19th-century geologists suspected the presence of this golden treasure house, in spite of the rich finds of the Lowveld, and its discovery in 1886 by two itinerant diggers was by sheer chance. George Harrison and George Walker were working as casual labourers on the farm 'Langlaagte' when, in search of suitable stone for the house they were building, they found that the rock contained traces of gold. The pair had stumbled onto the Witwatersrand's fabulous Main Reef (though neither benefited: Harrison sold his claim

for a meagre £10!), and within three years of this discovery the mining camp of Johannesburg had mushroomed into South Africa's largest town.

Visitors have a number of sightseeing options, among them underground tours of a working concern (**28**) arranged through the Chamber of Mines. More evocative of the early days is Gold Reef City (**29**), a marvellously authentic re-creation of pioneer Johannesburg built on the historic Crown Mines' site. Here one can explore the old workings (which yielded an impressive 1,4 million kg of the yellow metal during their lifetime), observe gold being poured and watch African traditional and 'gumboot' dancing. Among many other attractions are trips by steam train and horse-drawn omnibus, house museums furnished in period style, a Victorian funfair, replicas of an early pub, brewery, newspaper office, stock exchange, apothecary, cooperage and tailor's shop, and a variety of speciality stores.

Visitors in the early 1800s to the royal kraal of Shaka's Zulu empire wrote of the earth 'trembling' beneath the stamping feet of his *impis*, or regiments, as they executed the elaborate steps of rigidly-disciplined dances. Among all the black tribes of southern Africa, the innate sense of rhythm of their peoples found impressive expression in dance and song, whether it was ritual, narrative or recreational. The tradition has continued and when people – drawn from every tribe of the subcontinent – moved to the mines of the Witwatersrand, they brought their dances with them.

Such music as accompanies the dancers is provided by the often repetitive percussive hand-claps or chanting of the audience. Many Swazi dances are punctuated by the shrill whistle of the leader of each troupe (**30**), while others such as the amaZulu-ndlamu (**33**) beat a strict tempo with kerries on the small cowhide shields which they carry. In these all-male dances it is the leader who determines the routine not only of

the movements but also of the charac-
teristic high kick followed by stamping
in unison – the *indlamu* – in which the
ground literally shakes and which is
typical of Zulu dancing. Among the
Sotho, their colourful blankets and
conical straw hats contrasting sharply
with their western trousers (**32**), this
dancing is characterised by the vast
strides of the *mohobelo*.

Dancing often begins spontaneously,
even among miners coming 'off-shift' at
the end of a day spent underground. The
spectacular 'gumboot dance' exemplifies
this. Tribal finery (**31**) of shields, neck-
laces and resplendent ostrich-plumes is
reserved for the organized dances.

33

34 △　**35** ▽

Where most of Gauteng's mineworkers and urban poor find their weekend recreation in soccer and in dance, their more affluent fellow citizens swarm to man-made and natural pleasure resorts – often several hours' drive away. Among the most popular of these, and almost equidistant from both Johannesburg and Pretoria, is the Hartbeespoort Dam (**34**). Fed by the Crocodile and Magalies rivers, the dam was one of the first built in the North-West Province. Its wall has been heightened several times so that when full it covers 1 620 ha and sustains 15 000 ha of intensively cultivated land.

But agriculture is far from the minds of the crowds of weekend pleasure-seekers who throng its banks. Anglers young and old try to tempt the bass and carp with which its waters are stocked. Others enjoy sailing and waterskiing, for which there are abundant facilities. And ever along the shoreline drifts the tang of a hundred *braaivleis* fires.

At the weekend, throughout middle-class South Africa, the cult of the *braaivleis* reigns supreme (**36**). From patches of open veld to the manicured gardens of mansions and small suburban back-yards, the woodsmoke rises, bearing the aroma of grilling chops, steaks and *boerewors*, literally 'farmer's sausage'. And, as with any other cult, there are numerous schisms – almost every suburban South African male (for 'braaing' is 'man's work') is the ardent acolyte of the merits of a particular wood, temperature or spice best suited to his sacrifice. And – at least among those Afrikaners living north of the Vaal River – no *braai* is complete without an accompanying dish of *pap*, highly-spiced mealie-meal porridge prepared in three-legged cooking pots, of which the women are the cult's handmaidens (**35**).

Here too, the merits of recipes are argued hard and long. Indeed, the cult of the *braai* generates enough heated exchanges to fill a hot-air balloon on numerous crossings of another popular pleasure area – the Magaliesberg (**37**).

38△   39▽   41▽

40▽

Where Johannesburg is
brashly and busily dedi-
cated to finance and
commerce, Pretoria is
more sedate, its even pace fitted to that of
the thousands of civil servants and many
diplomats for whom – for much of each
year at least – this city is home. Pretoria is
the country's administrative capital –
dedicated to the business of government.
Surrounded by hills over which its
residential suburbs and admininstrative
buildings have gradually crawled, the city
is also the home of the world's largest
university teaching exclusively by
correspondence. From its starkly-modern
headquarters on Muckleneuk Ridge (38),

43△   44▽

◁
42

each year the University of South Africa provides courses for over 60 000 students drawn from the entire subcontinent.

But it is the Union Buildings (**42**) which dominate Pretoria. From their imposing site on Meintjieskop they are visible from every corner of the city. Designed by Sir Herbert Baker and largely in the Renaissance tradition, the two main sections, linked by Grecian colonnades, surround an amphitheatre from whose central steps the equestrian statue of General Louis Botha, first prime minister of a united South Africa, surveys a swathe of landscaped gardens.

While the Union Buildings are the embodiment of Pretoria, Church Square (**39, 40, 41**) remains its heart. Tranquil now and rimmed by buildings both old and new, it was here that the ox-wagons of the Voortrekkers were outspanned when they gathered in February 1857 for the dedication of the small thatched church which was Pretoria's first building. Here too, on the following day, these early pioneers – symbolized by the brooding bronze statue of a watchful farmer, rifle in hand (**39**) – cheered the first unfurling of the *Vierkleur*, flag of the youthful Zuid-Afrikaansche Republiek. It was this tiny republic which only a few decades later, under the leadership of President Kruger, was to defy the might of the British Empire.

Today the top-hatted statue of 'Oom Paul' Kruger (**41**) dominates Church Square as once he dominated the Afrikaner people in his largely-successful attempts to weld them together to become a single united nation.

An air of such history pervades much of central Pretoria and touches even its most modern buildings. Bronze busts of all the country's white leaders, including former premier J.G. Strydom (**43**), abound in the centre of the city, forming a link between the past and present. And this link, this sense of history, is at its most tangible in the Voortrekker Monument (**44**) which caps a hill a few kilometres from the city.

46 △   47 ▽

◁ 45

In its early years Pretoria was known as the 'City of Roses'; not only did every garden of its often-gracious homes boast a rose bed, but ramblers sprawled over hedges and fences. Today it is the 'City of Jacarandas', its wide streets lined with more than 70 000 of these spectacular flowering trees (45). Many are the descendants of two jacaranda trees – Pretoria's first – imported from Rio de Janeiro in 1870 for the then princely sum of £10. October and November is jacaranda time when masses of trumpet-shaped flowers transform the leafless branches of each tree into a lilac-blue haze and the falling blossoms carpet the ground as if in competition with the sky.

Jacarandas dot the city's many gardens and parks too, the oldest of which, Burger's Park, was the first piece of land in southern Africa set aside specifically as a park and botanical garden. Opposite it stands Melrose House (46, 47), typical of the imposing homes of wealthy Pretorians at the turn of the century. Today it is a historical museum. The interior of the stately dwelling, built by the owner of a stage-coach line, has little changed since 1902 when, as the head-quarters of Lords Kitchener and Milner, its dining room (49) was the venue for the signing of the Treaty of Vereeniging which ended the second Anglo-Boer War and set South Africa on its first

hesitant steps towards union as a nation. The table (centre) at which the treaty was concluded bears a silver plaque on which are engraved facsimiles of the signatures of all who signed the treaty.

The furnishings of the dining room have remained virtually unchanged since that momentous May day and the ghosts of the doughty republican Boers and their equally intractable imperialistic opponents still seem to crowd the table.

If there are ghosts, one of these will be the shade of Jan Christiaan Smuts, a delegate to the peace negotiations and later one of South Africa's best-known statesmen. Though an international figure in the decades which spanned two

48△   49▽

World Wars, General Smuts was essentially a simple man and it was to the rustic simplicity of Doornkloof (**48**) at Irene, near Pretoria, that he would return to relax and meditate in times of stress. He was also the guiding mind at the birth of both the League of Nations and the United Nations.

Although the shade of Paul Kruger looms over the 'Jacaranda City', it is Smuts who, more than any other South African, typifies Pretoria's spirit. He was a happy blend of academic and administrator, of soldier and statesman – and having fought to defend the Afrikaner republics, battled with equal dedication to unite Boer and Briton.

50 ◁   51 △   52 ▽

If South Africa is synonymous with gold, so to investors the world over gold has become synonymous with Kruger-rands (50), the one-ounce gold coins which, since 1967, have joined the British sovereign and the French gold franc as the small man's portable form of savings and a hedge against inflation. Marketed at a price slightly above that obtaining for gold, the coins are struck (51) at the South African Mint, in Pretoria, from blanks from the Germiston refinery.

The blanks are washed and polished (52) before being placed in the die where, in the case of 'proof' coins, they are struck twice. The proof Krugerrands, which sell at a higher premium, are essentially collectors' pieces, snapped up by numismatists and, because a limited number are minted each year, there is usually a waiting list of would-be purchasers. These coins are more carefully sorted and handled (53) to ensure they are free of blemish and, literally, in 'mint condition'.

Since the first Krugerrands were struck, more than 40 million of these gold pieces have been minted. In the record year of 1978, the 6 096 980 coins produced accounted for one quarter of the country's entire gold output. The obverse of each coin bears a portrait of 'Oom Paul' Kruger, from whom the coin takes its name.

54△ 55▽

In the *domba*, the culmination of the rites which mark the transition of Venda maidens from childhood to maturity, religion and culture create an aesthetically pleasing spectacle (**54**). This is the python dance in which both the serpentine file of participants and the undulation of their arms in accompaniment to the steps represent the great snake. The tempo is guided by the bass reverberation of a large wood and hide drum, creating a rhythmic tattoo as timeless as the ritual.

The *domba* is the climax of a period of initiation during which the young girls and boys of each Venda village spend several years as part-time inhabitants of a 'play village'. Here they elect their own elders and council and, to a great extent, mirror the pattern of adult routine in preparation for later life.

Tsetse-fly infested much of the area around the Soutpansberg in the Northern Province where the Venda people settled, so they are one of the few black tribes to whom the 'riches' of

56△ 57▽

58▽ 59▽

cattle-breeding were denied. Instead they became expert smiths, and the iron artefacts which they forged became both symbols of wealth and objects of trade. They have retained their tribal identity to a far greater extent than the once-powerful Ndebele, a tribe which has been largely absorbed into urban life. The colourful murals of Ndebele homes (55) are nevertheless a feature of the landscape of the south-eastern Highveld. House-painting, once executed in natural pigments but today far more likely to come from a tin, remains 'women's work', as do brick-making (59) and the spreading of the mud-dung mixture (58) which paves living areas.

The dark green and lush softness of subtropical vegetation and the stark multicoloured slashes of sandstone cliff vie for the eye's attention through much of the province of Mpumalanga. An African Garden of Eden, many parts of the area retain an unspoilt, primeval quality. Nowhere is this more apparent than in the upper reaches of the Blyde River Canyon (**60**) where, over many thousands of years, rushing waters have carved a winding path through dolomite and sandstone. In places the canyon is 1,5 km deep, and presents a spectacle which is at once awesome and beautiful.

But in parts of this Lowveld paradise man has battled with Nature, winning rich pasturage (**61**) and ordered forests from the gentle slopes of the northern fingers of the Drakensberg massif.

When gold was first discovered over 100 years ago in this part of Mpumalanga, malaria decimated the inhabitants of several mining camps. Today the miners are gone, but echoes of the past remain in names such as MacMac Falls (**62**). This 56-metre-high cascade took its name from a nearby mining village, whose inhabitants were so predominantly Scots that, when visiting the area, Transvaal's President Burgers dubbed it 'MacMac'. Although man has made his mark, there are parts (**63**) where the red spears of aloes form a barrier to say: Man go no further.

▷
66

64△   65▽

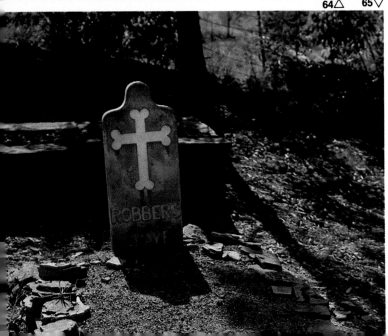

Much of this part of Mpumalanga was opened up by an international motley of miners, for the pioneer trekkers – the first whites to reach the area in any numbers – moved on, seeking more open, disease-free grazing for their herds. Even the black tribes were daunted by the malarial hazards of the lower-lying parts, so that the land lay unwanted – until the discovery of gold. The first strike, at Eersteling to the west in 1871, sparked a stampede of diggers. And prospectors wise in the experience of the Australian and Californian goldfields soon probed eastward, tracing the watercourses towards the probable source of the alluvial deposits. In the decade which followed, innumerable deposits of gold were found; some were worked for only a few weeks before their riches were exhausted, others continued to provide a handsome harvest of the precious metal for many years. Around the latter, towns such as Pilgrim's Rest (**64, 66**) soon developed from the tented camps of the early diggers.

Alluvial gold was found near here in a tributary of the upper reaches of the Blyde River in 1874, and within weeks a tent town of over 1 500 prospectors had mushroomed, fed by the relatively easy access of the established wagon route from Delagoa Bay to the Lydenburg mines. This was the 'road' made famous by Sir Percy FitzPatrick and today a memorial to his *Jock of the Bushveld* is situated 5 km outside the town. If the wagon route gave easy access for diggers and prospectors, it also provided easy pickings for bands of desperadoes who preyed on individual miners and armed wagon trains. Some met a swift fate (**65**), others escaped to eventual respectability.

The temptation was great. One nugget weighed 7,8 kg, earning its finder a paltry £750 compared to the R350 000 it would fetch today; legend has it that in one day enough dust and nuggets were recovered from one of Bourke's Luck potholes (**67**) to allow its finder to retire wealthy. The last gold was mined at Pilgrim's Rest in 1971.

68△   69▽

The streams and rivers fed by the waters of the Drakensberg bore wealth other than gold, laying down rich deposits of arable land and still providing irrigation for a wide range of agricultural produce. Tea has become an important crop, and vast plantations carpet the countryside in a rich harvest-time green (**68**) between Tzaneen and Barberton, yielding enough of the tender tips to brew more than 125 million cups.

And, though the crags and the canyons have remained immune to the plough, many of the slopes and hills of Mpumalanga have been given over to intensive forestry. The tangled indigenous woods have been replaced by orderly lines of imported trees – mainly pine and eucalyptus (**69**) – which feed the industrial needs of the nation. But pockets of primal forest remain, the haunt of colourful birds and other fauna which teemed here before their habitat was eroded as man fought to win the land from Nature. Nowhere has the victory been easy and it is only in the last century that the anopheles mosquito and the tsetse-fly have been driven from the lower-lying lands.

When the first trekkers reached the area the hills and plains were alive with game, and early records tell of 'herds of antelope stretching as far as the eye can see'. It was also here that the *rinderpest*

70▽

epidemic first struck, decimating those herds and practically eliminating the country's buffalo population. The disease began its onslaught in 1896 and in the next two years destroyed over 2,5 million cattle, as well as hundreds of thousands of antelope and other game. A locally-developed vaccine finally brought the epidemic under control and in 1903 it was eliminated from southern Africa. The cross-breeding of surviving cattle – like these being herded kraalwards near the Lebombo mountains (**70**) – with new imported strains has led to South Africa's livestock industry comprising more types than are found in any other country. Many of these new breeds are exported.

71△　72▽　73▽

The rocky fingers which splay west and north from the eastern mountain spine of South Africa's border with Mozambique provide some of the country's most spectacular scenery. The outcrops of the Lebombo range are studded with such sites as God's Window and World's View which provide travellers with the panoramas so explicit in their names. Rolling hills and plateaux are rent by sudden gorges (71) whose cliffs are veiled with tenacious trees and undergrowth. Beyond them Africa seems to stretch forever. So splendid and abounding with natural beauty is the area that one scenic drive has been dubbed 'the Panorama Road' and from it several spectacular cascades, including Lisbon Falls (72), can be reached. Typical of the tortuous roads which wind through the area is the Saddleback Pass (73) which climbs from Barberton to Havelock – one of the world's major sources of asbestos – on the Swaziland border.

Nearby lie the vast citrus estates of Zebedelia, established soon after World War I and, with over 650 000 productive trees, arguably one of the world's largest orchards. At harvest time the scent of oranges lies heavy in the air, a constant reminder that one is never far from subtropical fruits when in the Lowveld. Many roadside stalls (74) attest further to the agricultural riches of the region.

75△   76▽

74▽

Wild bananas, paw-paws and other tropical fruits already flourished in this vicinity when the first Trekkers passed through, for several such exotic fruits had been introduced to this part of Africa centuries earlier by slave traders. That eastern fruits survive here is underlined by the tremendous success which post-war plantings of litchi trees have met – the orchards near Kaapmuiden produce more than enough of this delicacy to permit its export.

Known by the people of the area as *Emanzana* ('healing waters'), Badplaas (**75**) is a popular recreational resort. Covering approximately 2 000 ha, the spa is centred on a series of hot sulphur springs, and is the best-known of several such mineral baths which occur in the area. Declared a health resort for the 'everlasting use of the public' in 1893, Badplaas is today a self-contained township. Its hotel, rondavels and large camping areas draw thousands of holidaymakers each year, particularly in winter when cooling winds allow the heat and humidity of summer to be temporarily forgotten.

Then, even the lush subtropical valleys seem briefly temperate; the thorn trees and rank grasses which fringe the hillside roads are sere, the air crisp, if dusty. It is at such times and against such backdrops that the donkey seems in his element.

This unjustly-derided animal – contrary to popular belief, the donkey is neither stupid nor lazy – helped open up the hinterland of the subcontinent, particularly in the humidity of the Lowveld.

Its immunity to diseases which debilitated and often killed other beasts of burden made the donkey, first introduced to southern Africa in 1656, an ideal and reliable form of transport for the early explorers and miners. Even though donkeys lacked the sheer pulling power of the oxen which comprised most trek-wagon spans, they accompanied most treks – as ubiquitous then as they are on the Lowveld's roads and dusty trails today (**76**).

77◁

78△   79▽

Today internationally renowned as a superb game sanctuary and a major tourist draw-card, the Kruger National Park had an uneasy birth. When the first white men reached the Lowveld it was an animal paradise, home to vast herds of antelope, elephant, giraffe and the range of predators which accompany such game. However, the high prices which ivory commanded in Victorian Britain soon led to the decimation of the elephant population and there was wholesale slaughter of other game too. One hunter claimed to have shot more than 600 springbok in one day – for pleasure and for the pot. By the late 1880s it seemed that game might be obliterated from the Lowveld and in 1889, though hunting was very much part of the Afrikaner way of life, the Transvaal *Volksraad*, or parliament, banned hunting in certain areas. The move was largely ineffectual and it took almost a decade before land was set aside between the Crocodile and Sabie rivers as a sanctuary.

However, before any suitable administrative structure could be established, the Anglo-Boer War intervened, and it was not until 1902 that practical steps were taken to establish what was then known as the Sabie Game Reserve. Many of the animals which survived the *rinderpest*

80△

81▽

died under the guns of Boer and British soldiers, so that when James Stevenson-Hamilton was appointed as first Chief Game Warden very little game remained.

Given the nickname *Skukuza* 'he who scrapes clean' by his black game rangers, Stevenson-Hamilton was to guide the destiny of the 19 019 km² park and its animal inhabitants for the next 44 years. One of the first steps he took was to announce that no shooting would be allowed in the park, and he formed a team of five white and 50 black rangers – the first of his troops in the unceasing war he was to wage against poachers. Within a year he had successfully prosecuted a group of senior police officers who had hunted game in the park. And though the main offender was fined only £5, *Skukuza* had shown that he meant business. Today, largely as a result of Stevenson-Hamilton's efforts, the park is home to a vast cross-section of African wildlife. Giraffe, the world's tallest animals (**77**), sweep sedately through the thorn-scrub in much of the park, sometimes falling prey to lion (**78**), though the king of the veld (**80**) is more likely to prey on one of the many types of antelope such as the massive 300 kg kudu (**79**), whose 1,5 m horns are not always a match for predators. The shy duiker (**81**) is too small for his regal attention and is left to other carnivores.

82△   83▽

Though the original boundaries of the Kruger Park were formed in part by rivers where the semi-aquatic hippo gambolled (**82**), animals are no respectors of man's delimitations and until recently the sanctuary's 950 km perimeter has been fenced with cable and barbed wire – as much to keep intruders out as to keep the animals in. But cables and fencing have meant little to troupes of chacma baboon (**83**) whose scavenging habits around the rest camps have earned them a reputation as pests. Nor has the fencing effectively deterred the elephant (**84, 85**) which have returned to the park and so bred that they must be culled. When the park was established the activities of poachers had driven these, the largest of all land mammals, away from the Lowveld. Stevenson-Hamilton recorded the thrill he experienced when he discovered that elephant had returned to the area. He had come upon them early one morning while walking along the river bank and thought, initially, that the two bulky objects in

84 △   85 ▽

86 ▽

the water were large rocks, only realizing that they were elephant when they moved – and then remembering that there were no rocks along that particular stretch of river.

Elephant are destructively voracious feeders, consuming as much as 250 kg of grass, shoots and stripped bark each day and thinking nothing of toppling a tree to reach a few tender morsels at the top. Confined as they are within the park, the havoc which they wreak on the vegetation deprives many other animals of sustenance. In recent years their numbers have become so great that their feeding habits have threatened the delicate ecological balance of the browsers and grazers which comprise the bulk of the park's animal population.

The question of grazing in the park is the subject of ongoing research, for not only has the elephant population exploded, but the numbers of predators – lion, leopard, cheetah, hyena and wild dog – also appear to be following an upward trend. This development has been linked to grassland being replaced by bush, thus making prey easier to stalk and the predator's young easier to feed. The park is also the home of innumerable birds, and some 400 different species have been recorded – including the pied kingfisher (**86**), seen here outlined against a rising moon.

87△ 88▽ 89▽

90▽

The days when the African plains teemed with game are over, and the mass migrations when animals in their hundreds of thousands moved across the Lowveld are no more. But on a daytime safari from one of the rest camps (**88**) in the Kruger Park one can still thrill to the sight of a herd of zebra, their ordered ranks broken by a lone springbok ram (**87**). There are around 20 rest camps in the park, providing varying degrees of accommodation in terms of comfort. All are fenced to protect the visitor from predators, and some are noted for the preponderance of certain species of game in the area. Both the Satara and Lower Sabie camps, for instance, are noted for lion, while in the northern area of the park, Letaba and Shingwedzi are regarded as the most likely places to sight elephant. The Marabou stork (**89**), however, is common throughout the park, its large ungainly body often an indication that the remnants of a kill are present in the bush.

Its bald head and neck, combined with its huge powerful bill, make it something of a nightmare figure, and the fact that it is often found sharing a feast of carrion with vultures does not enhance it in the minds of most visitors. Yet such scavengers play a vital role as the 'dustmen' of the veld, putting the final tidy touches to the remains of a carcass which may have already provided a meal for a lion family, wild dogs and hyenas. Their size, strength and the immense boss of their horns (**90**), which they can wield with devastating accuracy, ensure that buffalo seldom provide a meal for lions; the elegantly graceful waterbuck (**91, 93**) is more likely to do so.

91▽

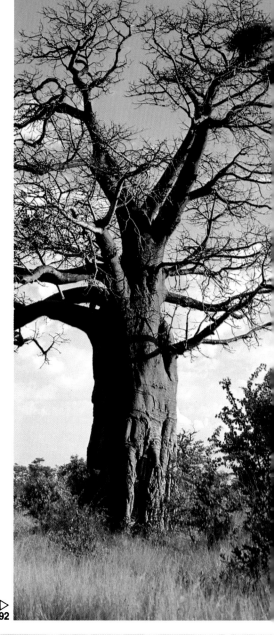
▷
92

93▽

In the drier regions of the park the huge and grotesque baobab (**92**) is found. Its grey trunk with tapering branches is claimed by many black tribes to be the result of God having planted it upside down. Baobabs develop a tremendous girth and one recorded by the missionary David Livingstone measured about 25 m around its base.

A deciduous tree, the baobab bears big, scented flowers which are thought to be pollinated by bats. These flowers are followed by large egg-shaped fruits containing a white pulp with a sharp 'cream of tartar' flavour which, when mixed with water, provides a refreshing and cool drink.

94△ 95▽ 97▽

96▽

In the Free State, part of the vast semidesert plateau which forms a great deal of the South African hinterland, kilometre seems to follow endless kilometre into a deceptive nothingness. Deceptive, because this largely unprepossessing tract of land is the nation's bread-basket. Its rich soil is given over in the east to the production of maize and potatoes on a scale unparalleled in Africa. To the west the steady encroachment of the Karoo has created dust bowl conditions in places, and intensive agricultural research has been devoted to finding a solution to the threat of a desert developing. Vast fields

of sunflowers (94) have been planted and these not only help to rehabilitate the soil, but also provide a valuable crop.

The land tends to be flat, broken only occasionally by low hills or koppies, but Nature seems to compensate for this in the richness of autumn tints with which she adorns the rural landscape. Small catchment dams are frequent, their moist presence indicated by the ubiquitous willow trees (95) while tall rows of the Lombardy poplars stand sentry over the remote fields (97).

If Nature has blessed the Free State landscape with poplars and willows, their warm colours breaking the monotony, she has saved the richest russets of her

▷
98

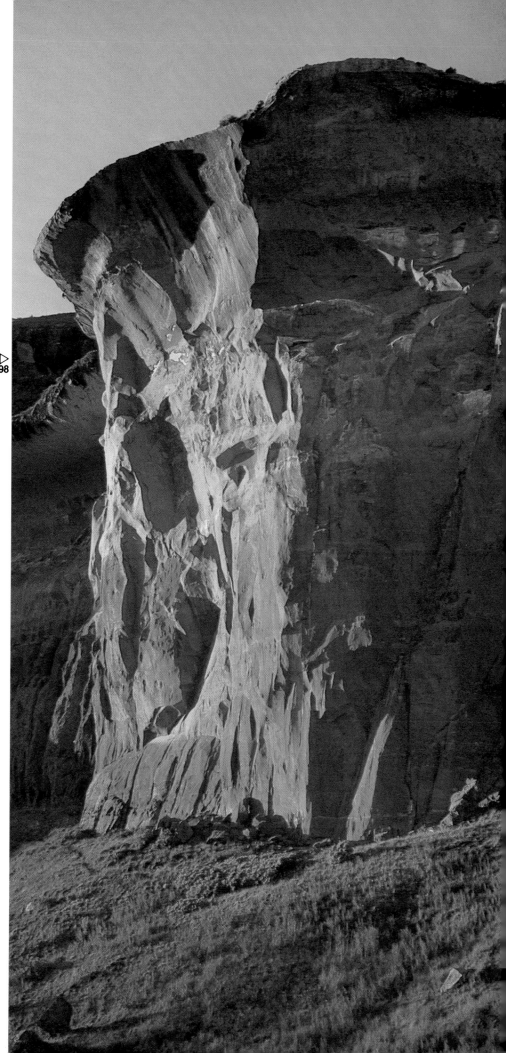

palette for an overpoweringly rugged outcrop in the north-eastern part of the province. The Golden Gate (**96, 98**) is spectacularly formed of twin peaks set in a massive cliff face. The brilliant range of oranges, yellows and reds which sweep in broad bands across the face and girdle the peaks are the result of many thousands of years of interaction between iron oxides present in the rocks. The area surrounding the Golden Gate forms a national park which provides access to the Republic's highest plateau, and the park itself has been restocked with many of the animals which were indigenous to the area – the white-tailed gnu, Burchell's zebra and the oribi.

99△ 100▽

A precipitous wall of rock, its jagged tips often hidden behind clouds, greeted the first white settlers as they pushed eastward from the Free State with their ox wagons in search of a route to the fertile lands of the Zulus and the well-watered Tugela basin. This wall was the central and most stubborn section of the Drakensberg, or 'Dragon mountain', and it took months of weary trekking before, with their slow and cumbersome wagons, they found a route through the mountains, following what is known today as the Oliviershoek Pass. It was also to take many decades before this section of the mountain

massif was tamed and eventually the Sani Pass linking Lesotho and KwaZulu-Natal was opened.

The Drakensberg is South Africa's largest mountain range, stretching from gentle beginnings in the Eastern Cape in a broad 1 064-km sweep to the north and west, finally to peter out in the empty wastes of Namaqualand. But it is with the contorted peaks of the eastern section that the 'Dragon mountain' is associated. Here the unparalleled grandeur of

soaring rockfaces in the vicinity of Giant's Castle (99, 101) is underlined by the wealth of flora which carpets the lower slopes of the mountains. The rugged wilderness of the scenery is a fitting setting for the Cape vulture (100) and other raptors which prey on the inhabitants of the kloofs and krantzes.

Giant's Castle, though not the tallest of the Drakensberg peaks – Injasuti is over 200 m higher – towers to a huge 3 314 m and is one of the country's major mountaineering challenges. The naming of this peak is attributed to Captain Allen Francis Gardiner, a naval officer turned missionary who probed the area in the mid-1830s while trying to

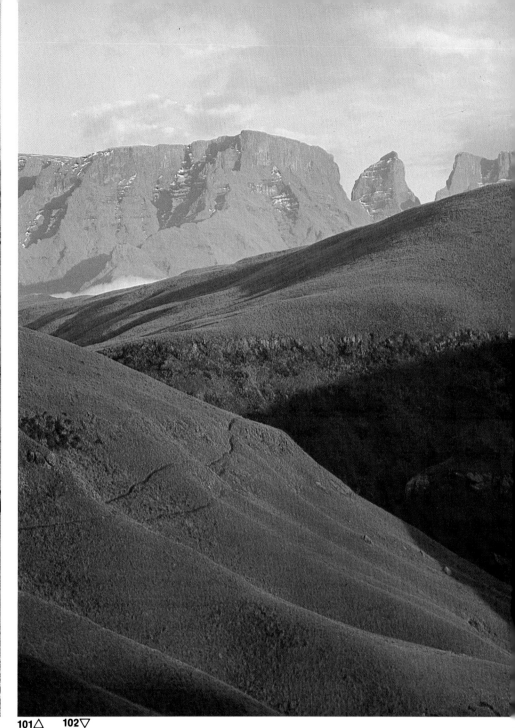

establish a mission station at the court of the Zulu king, Dingaan. According to Gardiner, the massive outcrop was a magnificent replica of Edinburgh Castle and the rock of its foundation. There certainly is a fortress-like quality about this particular peak which sets it apart. The determined missionary ventured into the mountainous vastness with only a small party, led by a Basuto guide and mounted on a sturdy and sure-footed mountain pony such as may still be seen throughout Lesotho today. This is still the surest method of transport on passes such as the Sani (102) and elsewhere in this land of winter snows, which has been dubbed 'the Roof of Africa'.

Tumbling streams, fed by melting winter snows and the high annual rainfall which the eastern Drakensberg enjoys, criss-cross the upland plateaux (**105**) to provide a fisherman's paradise of rainbow trout. But this busy rill (**103**) at the headwaters of the Tugela River plays a more significant role than that of providing sport for the visiting angler, and the catchment area is more important than catering for the parties of pony-trekkers (**104**). Aptly named Mont-aux-Sources by two intrepid French missionaries in 1836 (they trekked in from the west, across the hostile 'Roof of Africa'), it is the source of South Africa's three great rivers: the Orange, the Vaal and the Tugela, whose waters give life to much of the country's agriculture and industry.

In stark contrast to this part of KwaZulu-Natal, much of the Republic's hinterland has a low annual rainfall – indeed, one-third of its surface comprises semidesert. Thus the major rivers are all important to the economy, and dam construction has

107▽

108▽

had priority for many years. At the turn of the century inland irrigation schemes, fed by the mud and stone dams of the period, provided the means for intensive cultivation, and today modern technology with its accompaniment of even bigger dams has permitted the proliferation of this now vital method of agriculture.

Both the Orange and Tugela rivers rise within a few hundred metres of one another in the typical rock-girt grasslands of the high plateau (106); the Orange River drains to the north and the west on the start of a winding course which will take it 2 300 km to the Atlantic Ocean, a course during which it will be joined by the mighty Vaal River. The Tugela River's route is shorter, although it covers 560 km before reaching the Indian Ocean – a mere 220 km from its source. A substantial part of its volume is lost to the sea, in spite of a series of massive dams and other measures which were introduced to conserve its flow of 6 800 million litres per day. This is more than five times the volume of the Vaal River and, in flood, gives the river a strength which even in recent years has caused a great deal of destruction and has washed away road and rail bridges.

Water showing its more subtle force has honeycombed sections of the limestone strata, deep beneath the peaks, to provide a pot-holer's wonderland (107) of underground streams and caverns. Here, over hundreds of thousands of years, snow and rain have found their way into cracks and fissures, enlarging them into a smooth-walled labyrinth many parts of which remain unplumbed by man. That the upper portions of these caves and subterranean passages gave shelter to the ancestors of the modern speleologist is attested by many rich archaeological finds of Stone Age artefacts. More recently, within written memory, some provided homes for clans of San whose only memorials are the rock paintings which they executed in rich pigments – colours often still so fresh today as to vie with those of a mountain cloudscape (108) touched by the dying sun.

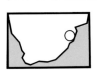

Considered to be the largest estuarine system in all of Africa, the Greater St Lucia Wetland Park is a 35 000-ha saline coastal lagoon which is fed by the rivers which drain northern KwaZulu-Natal and by water from the sea (109). Although it is very shallow, with an average depth of less than one metre, droughts take place every several years, causing considerable fluctuation in the water level: rivers stop flowing and a great deal of water is lost through evaporation, lowering the level to below that of the sea. As a result, sea water flows into the lagoon and under extreme conditions the salt from it

becomes so concentrated that in places the water can become three times as salty as that of the sea. Conversely, during wet cycles the lake level rises due to inflow from the rivers and the salinity levels consequently drop.

The duration of the full wet-dry cycle is about a decade, and the constant changes in salinity and water levels in the lake result in a dynamic ecosystem. Indeed, in this meeting of the waters from the land and the waters from the sea a vast natural workshop has been created in which there is a fascinating interplay between marine and freshwater life. Every plant and animal occurring in the Greater St Lucia Wetland Park has a preferred range of salinity within which it thrives and beyond which it dies: at low salinities submerged water plants thrive and form a food-rich habitat which attracts many ducks; at higher salinities the lake teems with estuarine

111△   112▽

113▽

fish and fish-eating birds. Some 6 000 white pelicans (**112**) breed in the northern wilderness of the lake while fish eagles, herons, gulls and terns are abundant. During periods of high salinity the plankton-rich water attracts as many as 60 000 flamingoes (**111**), whose pink masses create a spectacular sight.

A popular misconception is that the Greater St Lucia Wetland Park, because it is so shallow, is silting up. In reality, very little sediment enters the lake: the sediment-rich waters of the Mkuze River are filtered by the papyrus and reed beds in the Mkuze swamp north of the lake.

The Greater St Lucia Wetland Park remains one of South Africa's premier

angling venues. In addition, some of its 800 hippo (**110**), 1 500 crocodile (**113**) and several of its fish eagles can be observed from the 'Narrows'. A scenically beautiful drive along the Eastern Shores – the barrier between the sea and the lake – to Cape Vidal reveals 180-m-high coastal

dunes clad in luxurious dune forest, and grassy plains interspersed with wetlands harbouring reedbuck, kudu, waterbuck, buffalo and the elusive black rhino.

At Cape Vidal the sheltering reef protects a colourful diversity of fish, seaweed, corals and other marine life. North of here are the long stretches of golden beach for which this region is well known.

The Greater St Lucia Wetland Park is one of the three oldest reserves on the continent of Africa and its tremendous variety of scenery, habitat and plant and animal life has earned it recognition under the Ramsar Convention as a 'wetland of international importance'.

116▽

Though almost as many species of birds have been recorded at Lake St Lucia and its environs as in the entire British Isles and western Europe, these represent only slightly more than half of South Africa's avian population. More than 900 different species – or one tenth of all the world's known birds – have been observed in South Africa. The majority of these breed here and many are endemic. But statistics cannot begin to convey the magic of a carpet of lesser flamingoes, their deep pink plumage glowing like a sunset as they wade across a stretch of mud-flat, nor can they tell of the feathered glory of many woodland species such as this weaver (**118**) which,

when disturbed, takes to the air in a flurry of yellows and blacks. Even the apparent ungainliness of this immature pink-backed pelican (**114**), more prolific in the Greater St Lucia Wetland Park area than elsewhere in southern Africa, has its own special enchantment. Pelican, though cumbersome during take-off – their large webbed feet paddle frantically – have a winged grace of their own once airborne. In contrast, the jackal buzzard (**115**) is a masterful flyer, making graceful use of its powerful wings and broad tail to soar elegantly through the air.

The pelican's long, heavy bill which was immortalized by the humorous poet Ogden Nash, surmounts a soft naked

118▽

pouch which serves the dual purpose of 'netting' the fish and aquatic animals on which it preys, and holding these (**117**) until it is ready to eat them. Pelicans have refined cooperative effort to an artform when fishing, and dozens of the birds will gather together to form a semicircular line, beating the water with their large wings and feet to drive their quarry in front of them, where they can scoop up their prey in the lower half of their capacious bills.

Physical adaption, mirrored in the pelican's eating habits, manifests itself in a different way in the case of birds of prey, also known as raptors. The rare and endangered Cape vulture (**116**) has a powerful and sharp beak, evolved to allow it successfully to feed on the entrails of carcasses. Like pelicans, vultures will feed in packs, often fighting viciously over a meal. Vultures are, however, extremely fastidious and bathe daily, often flying considerable distances to find water in which to wash – a problem the pelican does not have to face.

Each midwinter, in a mysterious migration whose pattern has remained unchanged throughout written history, vast and concentrated shoals of two-year-old pilchards pass through the coastal waters of southern KwaZulu-Natal. Often this mass of fish is swept so close inshore and in such a density that beachfront housewives – and seemingly half the coastal population – rush into the shallows with baskets and basins to reap the silver harvest of the 'sardine run'. The excitement is so intense that otherwise-staid business executives have been known to discard their shoes and socks, roll neatly-pressed trousers above their knees and join the spray-filled fun. Others, more serious in their approach to the random harvest, use trek nets (**119, 122**) to haul tonnes of the fish from the surf with each trawl.

The sardine run, followed by a train of swooping seabirds as well as sharks and other large fish, disappears north of Durban and it is thought that the survivors of the winged, finned and two-legged predators are carried southwards to the Cape by the Agulhas current. Its waters, rich in a wide range of marine life, provide endless hours of pleasure for scuba-divers and anglers (**120, 121**) whose catches range from the mighty marlin and swordfish to the smaller species often sold in 'bunches' (**123**).

This broad spectrum of marine life provides tremendous potential for scientific exploration, and the Oceanographic Research Institute – the only such body in South Africa, which is privately-funded – probes KwaZulu-Natal's waters to harvest knowledge from the sea.

If the coastal and off-shore waters add to man's knowledge, the rich alluvial coastal plains of KwaZulu-Natal add to his or her girth. For these are the sugar lands (**125**) whose cane, first planted in 1851, has made South Africa one of the world's 'big five' producers of what was once known as 'white gold'. The warm humid climate and fertile soil of the hills

122△   123▽

124△   125▽

and valleys of the north coast are ideal for this towering relative of field grasses and, under KwaZulu-Natal conditions it gives one of the world's highest yields of sap. So intensive is the cultivation that even the steepest slopes are planted and here, where a tractor cannot hold its course, the planters revert to an earlier method of ploughing – with oxen (**124**).

The cane fields are among the world's last outposts of another earlier form of traction – the narrow-gauge steam locomotive. These old engines, several of them relics of the *eisenbahnen* of Germany's African colonies, carry the cut cane to the stamping mills where it is crushed and the sugar-rich sap extracted.

126△ 127▽ 128▽ 129▷

KwaZulu-Natal boasts a large number of popular game reserves, devoting nearly 250 000 ha to the conservation of its indigenous flora and fauna. It was from the thorny scrubland of its famous Hluhluwe-Umfolozi Park that the re-population of Africa with the white rhinoceros (**126**) began. This relatively placid giant – it is the smaller black rhino which has a deserved reputation for being aggressive – was once widespread throughout the savannas of southern and central Africa, its range extending as far as southern Ethiopia.

Rhinoceros horn – not actually a horn at all, but densely-compacted fibrous hairs – commanded princely prices in the Far East, where it was in great demand as an aphrodisiac. As a result, the white rhino was hunted almost to extinction. Its gentler mien – and the more open scrub in which it dwelt – made this stumpy-legged mammal a far easier target than its black relative. By 1930 very few were known to exist, and these were to be found only in the Umfolozi section, saved from extinction by the strictly-enforced preservation laws which had operated there since 1895. Slowly Umfolozi's pitifully small herds were built up and by 1960 the reserve faced the danger of overpopulation. This led to 'Operation Rhino', where white rhinos were reintroduced to other protected areas – first in South Africa and later in other parts of the world. The success of this project has allowed more than 4 000 rhino to be translocated.

Though Hluhluwe-Umfolozi proved a haven for the white rhino, KwaZulu-Natal's preservation laws were introduced too late to save the elephant, and in this part of South Africa the last tusker trumpeted his defiance of man in the 1800s. However, in 1981 elephants were reintroduced and a thriving population of over 170 of these magnificent animals can be found in the Hluhluwe section.

The diverse range of physical and climatic conditions which the province enjoys has not only contributed to the

preservation of other rare species such as the oribi, but has allowed most forms of wildlife that are indigenous to the sub-continent to flourish in one or other of the reserves. A wide range of aquatic

birds inhabit KwaZulu-Natal's lagoons and lakes, such as that at Ndumu (**127**); while impala (**128**) – renowned for their spectacular leaps when alarmed – are to be found in most reserves. So too is the brown hyena (**130**), a nocturnal scavenger whose powerful jaws can crush even the largest bones to powder. And though not numerous – they are a comparatively rare and endangered species even within the sanctuaries of all Africa's game parks – cheetah (**129**) inhabit most of the savanna reserves. Their skins are still prized as part of a Zulu warrior's regalia, though no longer as a symbol that the wearer has slain a specimen of this, the fastest predator in the world.

133△   134▽

131△   132▽

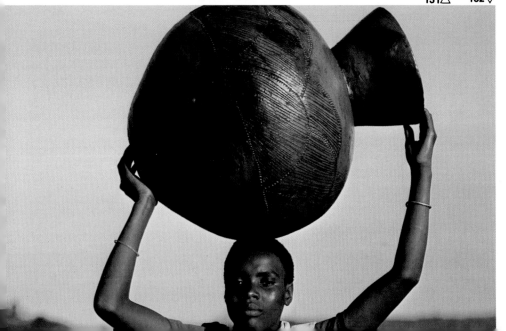

Where in the first half of this century KwaZulu-Natal was to ensure the continued existence of the white rhinoceros, the first decades of the nineteenth century saw the land spawn death. For this was the anvil on which was forged the Zulu nation and its military machine, an army responsible for human slaughter unprecedented in southern Africa. Entire tribes were annihilated by its onslaught – and it even withstood the power and might of Britain.

Today the Zulus are South Africa's largest single ethnic grouping and constitute approximately a fifth of the country's citizens. During the twentieth century so-called 'Native Reserves' were brought into existence in what was then known as Natal, and generally these were regions not suitable for commercial agriculture. The long term consequence of this was to create a patchwork of poverty and affluence in KwaZulu-Natal that will take a great deal of wisdom, patience and investment to even out.

Yet another consequence of this unequal division of land is that many people have had to seek employment in the urban areas of the country, mostly on the mines of the Gauteng province. It is mainly the men who go to the towns and for most of the year their wives, children and mothers are left to cultivate the fields and take charge of their rural homesteads. The fragmented 'Native Reserves' were constituted during the 1970s as the KwaZulu Homeland in accordance with the white Nationalist's 'Grand Apartheid' design. In the new South Africa these spurious political boundaries have been done away with and a united province of KwaZulu-Natal has been established.

According to Zulu tradition it is the womenfolk who are the basket weavers and to them fall the daily tasks of basket-work, brewing and moulding the often massive earthenware pots (**132** and **133**) used for the storage of nutritious beer, which plays an important role both socially and ritually.

When the tasks of daily living or the pastoral activities of the young herders are completed, both womenfolk and youths (**135**) set aside some time for beautification. The elaborate traditional head-dresses of the Zulu matrons are the result of long and painstaking effort. These colourful and intricate head-dresses are created from ochre and fibre, and the splendid coiffures are most often built up around a wooden framework, or may be structured from a tightly twisted 'rope' of cloth (**136**) to reveal its eventual inverted cone (**134**), given added glory by bands of extravagant beadwork, which may have a meaning or which may be purely ornamental.

More than any other of southern Africa's black peoples, it is the Zulus who have captured the world's imagination. Not only has the prowess of their warriors become legendary, but their noble bearing, enhanced by the richness of their tribal costume, has made them popular subjects for the illustrator since the earliest days of white exploration. Originally a vassal clan of the powerful Mthethwas, their rise to power began with Shaka, who assumed the leadership of the Zulus in 1816. Using this as a power base, he steadily gained control of the neighbouring 300 loosely-knit tribes and clans, forging them into a kingdom whose line of direct succession stretches unbroken to the present-day monarch.

Shaka, despot though he was to become, was both a brilliant administrator and military tactician. Developing the administrative system he had inherited from his predecessor, Shaka split the young men of the various clans into regiments according to age, instead of the previous family allegiances. In

doing so he ensured their loyalty to the throne rather than to the headsmen. These regiments literally grew up together, living in their own kraals with their own herds, and were forbidden to marry until they were 40 years old. Even then, the marriages were largely controlled by the King, who ensured that such alliances were with suitable women's 'regiments'. While no believer in sexual equality, Shaka regulated the lives of the Zulu women as closely as he did the men.

But such organized regiments, as many another militarist has found, require more than discipline and drill. Today's tribal dances (**139**) were part of the warrior's parade-ground routine. It served to keep them occupied when not being let loose on the surrounding tribes. In his army, each regiment or *Impi* was distinguished by its uniform and pattern of cow-hide shield. The short stabbing *assegai*, introduced to replace the spears which had previously been hurled from ineffectual distances, wreaked havoc in the hands of his warriors. Tribe

141▽   142▷

143▽

after tribe was conquered. Their chiefs were killed and the captives drafted into his army, while the women and children joined the losers' cattle as part of the spoils of war. In so developing his kingdom, Shaka annihilated entire clans and forced others to flee before military might in what became known as the *Mfecane*, or 'forced migrations'.

Shaka was assassinated in 1828, but in 12 short years he had forged the Zulu empire and created the legend that lingers today. And though his people have become westernized in terms of dress – so that even a royal hunt in which the tribesmen act as beaters (**141**) lacks the panoply of its past – there are events, such as tribal dances and displays (**137, 138** and **140**), when the magic of the legend is recaptured. And some customs, too, remain: single women still go bare-breasted (**142**) and only married women wear the elaborate ochre head-dress (**143**) which, like the rural beehive huts, is so much part of the traditional Zulu image.

At the beginning of every school holiday, or whenever there is a long weekend (in the South African context this is when a public holiday occurs, just before or after a weekend – preferably one at either end), the inhabitants of the northern regions embark on a mass exodus to the city of Durban on KwaZulu-Natal's coast. Its main attraction, the 'Golden Mile' (**144** and **145**), is a glittering 6-km-long stretch of seafront crammed with just about every diversion the hedonist could wish for. Here are amusement parks, pavilions, piers and pools, round-the-clock nightspots and fine eating places, emporiums and colourful markets, fountains, emerald lawns and graceful walkways. And, of course, acres of golden beach.

And for inland dwellers of the winter-dry Free State and Highveld the lure of the ocean is understandable. The heat and often cloying humidity is momentarily forgotten as one gapes in wonderment at the playful antics of the bottlenose dolphins at Sea World (home to the Oceanographic Research Institute) (**146**), or as one gasps in awe at the toothy menace of a Zambezi shark (**147**) in one of the giant tanks of the oceanarium. Many of the sharks on show have been rescued from special nets set offshore

146△

147△   148▽

along parts of the KwaZulu-Natal coastline to protect bathers and as part of an ongoing research programme, while income from the complex also helps to fund marine research.

But in spite of its pleasure-palace facade (**148**), Durban is a major industrial and commercial centre, and one of the southern hemisphere's busiest trade outlets. It was as a harbour that South Africa's third largest city had its beginnings: as Port Natal it saw the arrival in 1824 of KwaZulu-Natal's first white settlers. Today almost 40 million tonnes of cargo such as sugar, fruit, coal, anthracite, manganese and manufactured goods are processed by the dockyards.

149△ 150▽ 151△

Though Durban is the hedonist of South Africa's cities, it is also the most 'British'. Its centre is dominated by an unmistakably late-Victorian city hall which, with its palm trees and flower-sellers (**149**), has all the majesty of the 'Raj' – though not completed until 1910. To many, as they taken 'tiffin' on the cooler heights of Berea in subtropical gardens filled with the chatter of mynahs, it is still a last outpost of the Empire.

For nearly two decades after the arrival of the first white settlers in 1824, Britain wanted neither Durban nor KwaZulu-Natal – despite its naming in 1835 after the then Governor of the Cape. It was not until 1842, when the settlement had been absorbed as part of the early Boer Republic of Natalia, that Britain decided to annex the port and its surrounds. Even then they only did so to deny the Boers easy entry for arms and ammunition which the Cape authorities feared might be used against them, either by the hostile frontier tribes – with whom they were in constant conflict – or by the Boers themselves.

152▽

Today, catamarans on the placid beach (**150**) and the modern metropolis with its complex network of roads and railway tracks (**151**) reflect no legacy of those troubled times. But in 1842 it was here – where only four years previously the Trekkers had helped the small English settlement beat off Dingaan's *impis* – that the annexing forces were besieged by the Boers. In an epic ride, a young wagon-driver and lieutenant in the Port Natal Volunteers summoned help from Grahamstown. In ten days Dick King rode some 960 km to raise reinforcements from the frontier garrison and, returning by sea with the colonial troops, was acclaimed as the 'Saviour of Natal'. The troops then raised the siege – and went on to impose British rule in at least part of KwaZulu-Natal. Disappointingly, perhaps, the colourful and intricate war-like costumes of the city's ricksha boys (**152**) bear only a slight resemblance to the kilts of their fighting forebears – owing more to tourism than to tradition.

153△ 154▽ 155▽

The high-rise sophistication of Durban's seafront (153) is five centuries and a world away from the desolate swamp observed from afar by Vasco da Gama. And the modern craft in Durban's harbour bear only a remote resemblance to the trio of timber craft, headed by the *São Gabriel*, in which his expedition traversed these waters at Christmas 1497, to name the land they discovered *Terra do Natal*. There is no record that he landed here while establishing the sea-route to India. But long before the Port Natal settlement, other seafarers anchored in the waters sheltered by the Bluff, the first links in the chain of Durban's continuing maritime importance.

Despite the preponderance of pleasure-seekers who gambol among the ocean rollers (155) or take to the gentler waters of the Golden Mile's seafront (156), Durban is essentially a port city. Until the establishment in the 1970s of the massive minerals terminal at Richards Bay, 187 km to the north, Durban handled more annual tonnage than the combined total of all the Republic's other ports; the naval base at Salisbury Island – briefly abandoned after World War II but resuscitated in recent years – was one of the largest in the southern hemisphere, and its waterfront dives and nightclubs were notorious across the Seven Seas. Today the latter are the haunt of the

156 ▽

157 ▽

158 ▽

semisedate visitors rather than seadogs. Glittering disco-dancers have replaced their less reputable sisters of the earlier days. And Durban's seafront is graced by some of the world's most elegant hotels, many staffed by KwaZulu-Natal's Indians in respendent garb (154).

However, the same sea which gives its beneficence to the yachtsmen and bathers has its ugly side, and the waters off the coast of KwaZulu-Natal have claimed innumerable ships. It was from Durban in July 1909 that the *Waratah* sailed to her fate, giving rise to one of the sea's major, and still unsolved, mysteries. The twin-screw steamship, with luxurious accommodation for 100 passengers and a

crew of 119, was one of the largest and most modern on the run from London to Australia. On her second return voyage from Durban on July 26 she passed and exchanged flag signals with the *Clan McIntyre* on the following day; she has never been seen since. No wreckage or other sign of her has ever

been discovered and it is believed that the *Waratah* foundered in a freak storm, beaten into the maw of the deep by one of the giant waves for which these waters are notorious. Fortunately the forces which spawn such waves allow their mellowing before they reach the shores, and many stretches on this part of the coast offer fine surfing (158).

Thus it is as a pleasure-ground that its modern visitors remember Durban's seafront pool and playground (157) and its serried ranks of graceful yachts, its funland, its splendid sporting facilities, its luxury hotels and fine restaurants, many of which pay delectable tribute to the city's Indian heritage.

◁159 160△ 161▽

The Indians were 'visitors' to KwaZulu-Natal only in the sense that they were never meant to stay. The first to arrive in South Africa were indentured workers, brought from Madras to labour in the cane-fields of KwaZulu-Natal whose planters were faced with a chronic employment problem. The rich sugar crop thrived, but the local Zulus refused to tend the fields. Labour was sought elsewhere and, in the final weeks of 1860, 658 men, women and children arrived in Durban to begin a three-year stint in the plantations. They were the forerunners of a massive influx which 50 years later – when the importing of labour was brought to an end – was to see some 150 000 Indians established in KwaZulu-Natal. Today the province is the home of an estimated 800 000 of South Africa's over 1 000 000 Asian population, and descendants of the indentured labourers are among the leaders of the new South Africa. Provision was originally made for the workers to be repatriated at the end of their term of employment – which was extended first to five years and later, with freedom to choose their employer, to ten – but few of them wished to return to the poverty of their birthplace.

Most of these Indians were Tamil-speaking Hindus and Muslims, and they still comprise the bulk of the Republic's Asian population. However, their growing community also attracted a substantial number of Gujarati traders who soon established thriving businesses throughout KwaZulu-Natal, causing concern among their white counterparts who saw them as a competitive threat. It was to protect these Gujarati interests that a young Indian lawyer, Mohandas K. Gandhi, arrived in South Africa. And it was here, later, that as Mahatma and leader of the Indian political struggle, he developed his philosophy of passive resistance, or *Satyagraha*. That he overcame both prejudice and political power-play, in which the Indian was the controversial pawn, is part of South Africa's history. And the Indians' presence as part of the land's business

162▽ 163▷

164▽

and professional community is a measure of the first success of a philosophy which was eventually to win for India her independence and which was to spread around the world.

Many South African Indians maintain close links with their relatives in India, but even to those who do not, it still looms large as the source of their culture and way of life. Women still wear the graceful sari as they buy or sell the wares of the market (159), its airs redolent with the smells of curry and spices. At Durban's Grey Street mosque (160), the largest in the southern hemisphere, men and women still worship strictly segregated according to sex (161, 162). The splendour of oriental pageantry, alive in colour and equipage, still radiates from the Hindu festivals and ceremonies (163) celebrated throughout KwaZulu-Natal. Even the brilliance of a flower-seller's blooms (164) seem to echo the richness of the land to which the first poor labour force arrived, giving not only their expected sweat, but adding to the mélange of South Africa's cultures.

Its rolling landscapes often a seemingly-endless patchwork of tilled fields and pasturage (**165**), there is little in the former Transkei region today to remind travellers that here, less than 150 years ago, a 17-year-old girl led a powerful nation to the brink of suicide. Her name was Nonquase and she grew up in a rondavel with its surround of aloes very similar to those that dot the countryside today (**166**).

But Nonquase had a vision. She claimed that a great wind would spring up and bring forth ancestral warriors to drive the white man into the sea. To the Xhosa tribes, who had been engaged in a

167△   **168**▽

series of wars with the colonists for over 50 years, this was heady stuff. Even Nonquase's pronouncement that before the wind of change would blow they must kill all their cattle and destroy their grain, did not deter the tribesfolk. Herds were decimated, food was destroyed and, when the fateful day in 1858 arrived, nothing happened. In the famine which followed tens of thousands died, and Xhosa might was broken.

Poverty is still a factor in the land of the Xhosa and people have turned increasingly to the sea as a source of food (**167**). All along the wild beauty of this dramatic coastline (**167**) nature has provided a rich harvest of sea foods.

169△   170△   171▽

In 1976 the land of the Xhosa was declared the 'independent' Republic of Transkei by Pretoria. But the political manipulations of the past have brought few changes, either in the pattern or standard of living of the people. Poverty is a stark feature of the region and despite attempts by the social engineers of apartheid, who poured millions into the Transkei in an attempt to make it a separate and economically viable country, it still has very little industry and few jobs. As a result, people have to migrate to cities to find employment ... and those who remain behind wait patiently for their remittances in order to survive (172). Firewood is the main source of energy for most of the people and as part of their daily chores women and girls scour the hills for this precious commodity. They can be seen along the roads carrying bundles of sticks and twigs on their heads (169). Wood-gathering is only one of the many tasks which is the woman's traditional lot: she must also cultivate the fields and make her own domestic implements such as these simple brooms (173), as well as undertake all the normal chores associated with domesticity. The division of labour in traditional Xhosa society is well entrenched. The older women do the cooking and brew the beer while the younger women undertake the more energy-sapping chores. But in a land where poverty remains the norm and with more and more mouths to feed, the land has to be cultivated more often. As a result, soils become exhausted and barren and the erosive forces of nature create ghastly scars across the countryside (171). Contour-ploughing (175) is encouraged

◁172   173△   174▽

175▽

and it is assisting with the recovery of the land, but the problem of soil erosion remains serious. Pipe-smoking by women is an interesting custom among the Xhosa that comes with seniority (172). Married status is proclaimed by a swathe of turban.

Tending cattle and livestock is the main responsibility of the boys and youths in a tribal household. Cattle play a central role in traditional Xhosa society as they are the main measure of wealth and medium of exchange. The amount of *lobola* a prospective husband has to pay his father-in-law for the fertility rights of his daughter is measured in cattle. *Lobola* is an ancient custom that is

rooted deep in the social customs of many black people of the subcontinent. Many customs are slowly disappearing as urbanization and modernization take root. But among the Xhosa initiation ceremonies, in which circumcision plays an important part and marks the transition from adolescence to adulthood, are

still common. Initiates, called *abakwetha*, their heads shaved and their bodies painted with river clay (170, 174), live apart from the community in special thatched lodges. While the wounds of their circumcision heal, they are taught the mores and behaviour expected of them as adult members of society, and are taught tribal history as well.

At the end of their period of initiation, the thatched lodge – one of the few beehive structures which the Xhosa have retained from their earlier period – is ceremoniously burned and the *abakwetha* race each other to a river, to cleanse themselves of the clay. They have reached maturity.

176△ 179▷

177△ 178▽

Herding cattle meant that young boys spent many long hours in Nature's incredible classroom. Boys had to learn the lore of the veld to survive. Not only did they have to find their own food, such as these boys making their way to the rocky shore to find oysters and other shellfish (**179**), but they also had to understand the behaviour of birds (**179**) or other animals which may indicate the presence of danger.

The Xhosa, being part of the greater Nguni grouping, had a long-standing warrior tradition, and interclan conflict, fuelled by the imperatives of land and water for man and stock, was common. When white settlers arrived in this area the same imperatives applied and constant clashes between white and black resulted. The air of calm tranquility in the Amatola mountain range and the pastorally idyllic scenes which mark the land between the Great Fish and the Kei rivers (**177**) belie its history of bloody conflict that took place here during the late 18th century and much of the 19th. This was the land on which Phalo settled after a clash with his son, Galeka, which created two factions within the Xhosa nation and which many, many years later provided the motivation for the creation of two separate and independent national states – the Transkei and Ciskei – in Pretoria's apartheid policy. This division came about as a result of a bloody family quarrel that occurred more than two centuries ago. In the mid-18th century Galeka, heir to the Xhosa chieftainship, launched a rebellion against his father, Phalo. Loyalties were divided but Phalo, with the assistance of his favourite son, Rarabe, put down the uprising after a series of skirmishes in which both sides sustained heavy losses. Although Phalo and Rarabe were victorious, they made the decision to migrate with their supporters across the Kei River to create a geographical split in the tribe which continues to this very day.

The area in which the victors settled was the battleground on which a series of nine protracted clashes – known to history as the Frontier Wars and spanning more than a century – were fought. It was here that white and black, both hungy for land, first came into extended contact. And it was here too, in the shadow of the Amatola Mountains, that one of the most bitter of the wars broke out, and ostensibly for the pettiest of reasons. It began in 1846 with the ambush of a patrol sent to arrest a tribesman who had allegedly stolen an axe. The Xhosa chose this incident as an excuse to invade the Colony and made off with many head of cattle. In retaliation a punitive expedition of colonial forces, aided by tribes hostile to the Xhosa, set out but were hampered by drought. The Xhosa withdrew to the mountains, remaining undefeated until burgher forces invaded what used to be the Transkei and claimed for the Colony all the land west of the Kei River. The War of the Axe – though not the last of the Frontier Wars – was part of the gradual process which led to peaceful coexistence (178) between black and white in this part of the Cape.

The pincushion of the spires and steeples of more than 40 churches and chapels which prick its skyline has earned Grahamstown the nickname 'City of the Saints'. But 'City of the Sinners' might be no less appropriate, for half of the first stone structure built in this former garrison town was a gaol. During the unpredictable days of the Frontier Wars Colonel John Graham, who established the town as his headquarters in 1812, probably needed the cells as much for his 'rough soldiery' as he did for the Xhosas of the Zuurveld, where he had come to impose an uneasy peace.

His task of policing the vast tract of land between Algoa Bay and the inland mountain ranges, and containing the cattle-hungry Xhosa tribes behind an arbitrary eastern boundary, proved almost impossible. Time and again the blacks probed westward and threatened the Cape Colony. In these circumstances, and to provide a protective buffer, the British government devised a major

immigration scheme. This came to fruition eight years after Colonel Graham had established his garrison.

The arrival of the 1820 Settlers at Algoa Bay on April 20 is commemorated in one of several stained-glass windows (**182**) in the Methodist Church. St George's Cathedral (**180**) incorporates part of the original church – used as an ammunition depot and a refuge for women and children when Grahamstown was threatened in the 6th Frontier War of 1834-35. St John's Anglican Church in Bathurst (**183**) – the oldest Anglican church in South Africa to remain unaltered – served a similar use before it was even completed. The arrival of the Settlers had spurred the Xhosa to more frequent raids rather than deterring them, and for many years the brass bell of St John's (**181**) was as likely to call the local inhabitants to arms as to call parishioners to church.

Life was not easy for these early immigrants who left their indelible stamp not only on that part of the Eastern Cape still known as 'Settler Country', but on South Africa as a whole. Even though they were given free passage from Britain, were issued with seeds and implements at low cost, and were to be given title deeds for the lands they occupied, everything seemed to conspire against their success.

Severe drought, crop failure, floods in 1823 and constant attacks by the Xhosa throughout the first five years almost caused the collapse of the new settlement. However, the establishment of several forts and of villages such as Bathurst, then the administrative centre of the Zuurveld, was still made possible. An improvement in conditions from 1825 onwards marked the beginning of a prosperous era for the community.

Outside the 'locations', as the occupied lands were called, farms were bought and the hiring of black labour allowed expansion into pastoral farming. The wool industry flourished and skilled artisans practised their trades in the towns.

Churches were built all over the district, and schools and academies were started in towns like Salem and Grahamstown. The 6th Frontier War cost many lives and devastated the Albany District, as the Zuurveld had come to be known, but the survivors rebuilt their community. By 1864 the area was so stable and so important that the Cape Parliament held a session in Grahamstown – the only time it did not sit in Cape Town.

Today the hilltop site a few kilometres outside Bathurst, from which Col. Jacob Cuyler allotted 'locations' to the first immigrants, is capped by a topograph showing their sites in relation to the outspread (**184**) 'Settler Country'.

When the Portuguese cartographer Manuel Pe-restrelo, charged with charting the south and east coast of Africa, reached Plettenberg Bay in 1597 he named it Bahia Formosa, or 'beautiful bay'. It was not the first name bestowed on this curving stretch of shore, nor was it the last, but it was certainly the most appropriate. For Plettenberg Bay (**185**) – so dubbed by Governor Joachim van Plettenberg in 1778 thereby ending its multi-named confusion – is regarded by many as the jewel of the Garden Route.

This verdant expanse of lakes, rivers and forests stretches from Swellendam in

187△ 188▽

the west to Humansdorp in the east and is framed by the warm Indian Ocean and the rugged Outeniqua and Tsitsikamma mountains. And where Durban is the mecca of the frenetic pleasure-seeker, the estuaries and beaches of the Garden Route provide a tranquil retreat for the angler. He may cross the Storms River Mouth suspension bridge (**186**) to the privacy of seagirt rocks shared only with the seals – or seek a silent cove of sand.

Survivors of the shipwrecked *São Gonçalo* who spent almost a year on the shores of Plettenberg Bay before being rescued in 1630, saw the area as a lotus-land. Animals and wild fruits abounded in the primeval forests, there were fish

aplenty in the rivers and lagoons, and the climate was balmy. On a large slab of sandstone they carved the name Perestrelo had chosen, and though it has passed from usage, the stone remains with its words 'Bahia Formosa'.

Many parts of the lush Tsitsikamma Forest – which with the Knysna Forest covers 36 400 ha to form South Africa's largest woodland – have remained almost unchanged since then. In places it marches to the very edge of the shallow coastal cliffs (**187**). But the vast stands of yellowwood, stinkwood, ironwood and indigenous trees proved a magnet for the timber-hungry settlements of the Cape.

Ten years after Van Plettenberg had given the bay its permanent name, the sound of the axe replaced the call of the Knysna loerie to echo among the trees, and stacked baulks of timber lined the sands over which the luxury Beacon Island Hotel (**188**) today stands guard.

189△ 190▽

The timber wharves have long since disappeared from Plettenberg Bay and the wood and canvas of holiday-makers' deck chairs have replaced the spars and sails of the coasters. At Knysna – the other main source of beams and boards for the 19th-century building boom – timber and tourism go hand in hand. The placidity of its lagoon – a pleasure-haven for small craft and light-tackle anglers – is in sharp contrast to the angry currents and waves which pound the narrow entrance of The Heads (**189**). The sleepy-hollow weekday atmosphere of the town's main street gives no indication – save for the distant whine of a circular saw – that Knysna is also the home of

several factories, where some of the most expensive woods in the world are meticulously crafted into furniture.

For nearly 150 years Knysna thrived as a port as sailing vessels, and later coastal steamers, loaded timber from the dense forest. The first attempt to establish its viability as a harbour met with disaster when, in 1817, the transport brig *Emu* was wrecked while attempting the first crossing of the bar. But later efforts were successful and it was not until the 1950s that – under the pressure of cheaper rail transport – the port was closed, leaving the lagoon to smaller craft (**192**).

Vast forestry plantations (**191**) still cover the hills surrounding the lagoon. Nor has

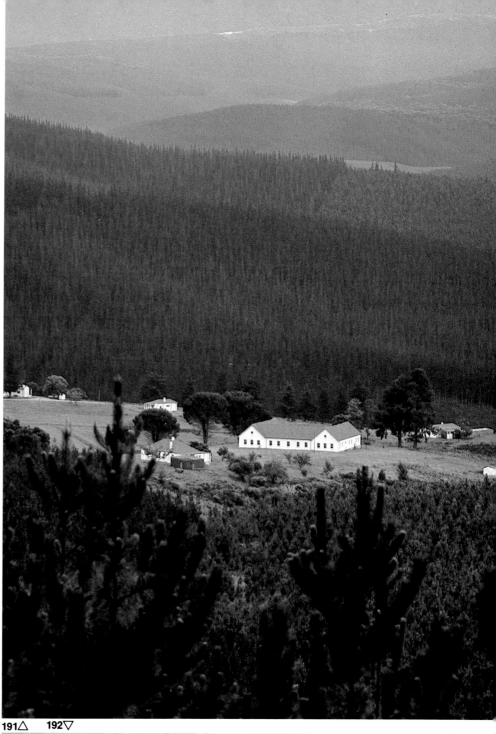

191△   192▽

the haven severed its links with maritime adventure. A thriving boat yard has built several internationally-renowned yachts, continuing an industry started by George Rex in 1830 when he built the first of Knysna's sea-going vessels. Rex, reputedly the son of George III from his morganatic marriage, was banished to the Cape. In 1804 he was granted the farm Melkhouts-kraal, on which Knysna developed, and lived there for 35 years until his death. He is, in fact, better remembered than his putative father, after whom the nearby inland town of George was named. It is on the road to George that the church of Belvidere (190) stands – referred to as Rex's church, but built after his death.

Beyond the ancient forests there is a softening of the land along the Garden Route, and a chain of lakes punctuates the littoral, separated from the sea by low brush-covered hills. Along this stretch, woody dells and reed-whispering waters vie with sparkling and seemingly endless beaches, such as that of the Wilderness (**193**). Shallow reefs sometimes fringe the headlands and are exposed at low tide, providing a bounty of oysters and other shellfish. The survivors of an early shipwreck on this stretch of coast recorded that they 'subsisted on a diet of oysters and rainwater for nigh six weeks' as they followed the shore westwards to reach the Cape.

195△

No one would envy the castaways their ordeal, but many might covet their menu – oysters harvested from the waters between Knysna and Mossel Bay have a justified reputation as the finest and sweetest in South Africa. But pollution and over-exploitation had devastated many of the original oyster-beds and these gourmet delicacies were becoming increasingly difficult to obtain when, in 1950, private enterprise and officialdom – in the shape of the Fisheries Development Corporation – stepped onto the stage.

Not far from the picturesque row of cottages which marks the entrance to Knysna (**194**), commercial oyster-beds were established. These today supply the tables of restaurants and hotels throughout the country; shipped live and still sold commercially by the gross – in spite of South Africa's metrication system – many even find their way to the sea-water tanks of hotels in other coastal resorts.

All along South Africa's coastline the sea offers up her riches, but there are others of which she appears miserly. One such treasure, until recently, was oil – a mineral which many geologists believed was present in economically workable quantities along the southern continental shelf, and one which the country's otherwise ore-rich treasure house has lacked (although South Africa did develop the world's first major viable oil-from-coal plant and remains the leader in this field).

To initiate and coordinate the search for the missing mineral, Soekor (the Southern Oil Exploration Corporation) was established in 1965 and funded to the tune of billions by a central government that was becoming acutely conscious of the international sanctions threat. During the early 1980s encouraging traces of oil and natural gas were discovered by the giant offshore drilling rig (**195**) in the sea-bed off Mossel Bay. Mossgas, the operating company, went into full production in 1990.

196△   197△   198▽   201▷

199△   200▽

Isolated from the mainland by 50 km or more of turbulent seas, the crews of the oilrig off Mossel Bay have none of the communications problems of the first visitors to this stretch of coast. A regular helicopter service keeps them supplied with up-to-date entertainment, newspapers and mail. Fittingly, this private postal method based on sophisticated technology sets off from Mossel Bay (**197**), for it was here that South Africa's first postal system – based on simple ingenuity – had its beginnings.

In May 1501, Pedro d'Ataide, the captain of a Portuguese ship not much larger than the sea-going fishing boats still built here today (**196**), put in to

Mossel Bay for fresh water. In a milkwood tree beside the spring where his crew filled their casks he hung a sea-boot containing a letter addressed to his home. Remarkably, the letter was found less than two months later and eventually reached its destination. D'Ataide's ingenuity was commemorated by the proclamation of the milkwood as a national monument in 1938. The 'Post Office Tree' was the precursor of what developed into a systematic, if irregular, postal service with engraved stones replacing the sea-boot as 'letter-boxes'.

It was to take more than three centuries before the seed planted by D'Ataide at Mossel Bay was to bear fruit inland. A small post office was established in Cape Town in 1792 to handle items between the settlement, Europe and the East Indies, but Hottentot runners carried official despatches to distant outposts. It was not until 1805 that regular mails began.

Post was delivered to the Drostdy – which served as both home and office of the local magistrate, or *landdrost* – and

was collected from here by inhabitants of the district. But the Drostdy – that at Swellendam (**198**) is a particularly fine example of Cape Dutch architecture – was much more than a mere postal depot or even courthouse: it was the administrative centre, records-repository and tax-collection office for vast tracts of territory. It was the focal point, too, of what little cultural life there was, so that it is appropriate that most Drostdys which remain today are museums – custodians of the treasures of the past (**200**) as once they were of taxes.

Today Mossel Bay is a typical coastal town, lifted from mediocrity by the oil terminal and tank farm of its port and linked to the outside world by a modern airport as well as rail and road. Steel and concrete bridges span gorges such as that of the neary Gouritz River (**199**), permitting a passage in seconds where progress once took days. But small boats still put to sea from here, and small boys still impatiently await the day that they will join their fathers on the fishing grounds (**201**).

202△ 203△

 Spectacular calcite formations of almost every known type stretch in a wonderland labyrinth of colour through the limestone strata beneath the Swartberg range. These are the Cango Caves and their full extent can only be guessed. Some 2,4 km of underground passages linking 28 chambers are open to the public, but speleologists exploring the maze of the Cango Caves system have discovered several other cavern chains – at least two of which are as large as Cango – and they believe that many more exist.

Subterranean water action over tens of thousands of years first scoured the honeycomb of chambers and passages. Then, in a much slower and gentler process, it carried the soluble calcium carbonate through tiny cracks and fissures to allow the formation of stalactites and the gradual build-up from the floor beneath them of stalagmites. Throughout the chambers of the Cango network many of these have ultimately joined to form imposing pillars (**202**), while elsewhere brilliantly coloured flowstone walls and spectacular curtains of calcite reflect the light (**204**) from strategically placed lamps. Rimstone pools, calcite flowers and straws, and helictites – which grow in all directions – add to the magic.

The caves were 'discovered' in 1780 by a farmer Van Zijl. Legend has it that one of his herders was searching for missing livestock when he stumbled on the entrance, later leading his employer there. His find is commemorated in the name 'Van Zijl's Hall' given to the largest of the chambers in the first series of caves. Here electric lights dispel the blackness to reveal a range of formations, at once grotesque and beautiful, which occupy a cavern 100 m long and 50 m at its widest. Even larger is the 'Wonder Cave', a splendid 270 m extension of the first system and discovered in 1972. Three years after this find another sequence of chambers 1,6 km long was

204▽

probed for the first time. Dubbed 'Cango Three', its extremely difficult access and potentially dangerous passages have prevented its opening to the public. However, speleologists (**203**) continue to explore its marvels.

Shortly after Van Zijl's discovery the Cape authorities claimed control of the caves, realizing even then the probable attractions of this natural wonder – in spite of the fact that the 'visitors' of two centuries ago could not probe very far, and tallow candles and weak lanterns served as their only illumination. An entrance fee was charged, trespassers were fined – though the inaccessibility of the caves must have made such a

transgression hard to prove or monitor – and the income derived from the caves was 'devoted to educational purposes'.

The late 18th-century explorers were not the true discoverers of the caves. San paintings near the main entrance indicate that it had been occupied by them. Stone artefacts – unlike those of the San – found inside the cave show that their forebears lived there 25 000 years ago, in the Middle Stone Age. Bats also appear to have made it their home from earliest times. The population has decreased, but at the rear of one of the chambers Cape horseshoe bats sheathed in transparent calcite indicate that they were once present in substantial numbers.

205△   206▽

Today rivalling the nearby Cango Caves as a tourist attraction, Oudtshoorn's ostrich farms (**205, 207**) bear mute testimony to a more gracious world than that of the 1990s – a world of bustles, plumed bonnets and feather boas, a world before the advent of the internal combustion engine. For it was the motor car which signalled the end of the ostrich feather boom, in whose final decade – from 1903 to 1913 – the wing and tail plumes of the world's largest bird earned South Africa almost as much as wool.

Indigenous to the continent and found throughout the drier parts of South Africa, the ostrich compensates for its inability to fly with prodigiously powerful legs that can carry it at speeds of up to 40 km/h and can deliver a lethal kick – a combination that allows it to evade most predators. Records show that ostrich-riding was a youthful pastime among early settlers – and it still provides a source of hilarity for visitors to a modern ostrich farm (**206**). But the bird's flesh was not particularly appetizing – usually there was tastier meat to be obtained from one of the many species of antelope – so that the ostrich was little hunted by the settlers.

Its eggs were, and still are, considered something of a delicacy. One ostrich egg contains the equivalent of two dozen hen's eggs, but they were not always easy

207△   208▽   209▽

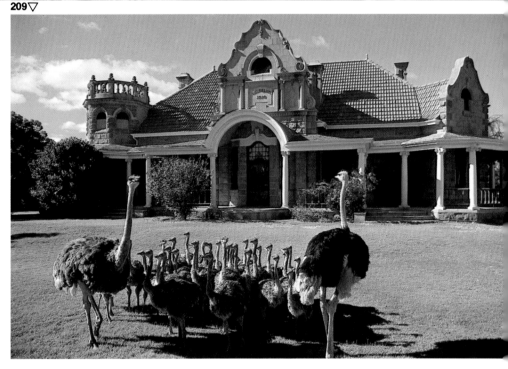

to find. The flecked brown feathers of the female provide splendid camouflage against the dry scrub of the veld during the day, when the hen sits on her clutch of 16 or more eggs. The black plumage of the male is an ideal night-time cloak when the cock takes over the role of incubation and guarding the nest.

The indigenous San used ostrich egg-shells to carry and to cache water. They also ground pieces of the thick, durable shell into disc-like beads thousands of years before the arrival of the white settlers. These strings of beads were not exclusively worn as a popular adornment by the San but were also extensively used by many of the black Bantu-speaking

tribes of the region. The latter also made use of ostrich feathers as part of their traditional ceremonial regalia.

But until the 1860s the ostrich went largely undisturbed – inflating his neck when angered (208), taking to his heels when threatened and subsisting on the meagre peckings of the veld. Then a sudden change in fashion in distant Europe gave the ostrich unexpected economic importance. Almost overnight the long plumes became an essential accessory in the milliner's craft, while the lesser wing feathers, or 'spadonas', were in great demand for feather boas.

To the farmer of the Little Karoo, scratching a meagre existence from the

land, the new vogue for feathers was a godsend. His stock was freely available in the veld and if he could catch a pair of ostriches, his only capital outlay was to fence a paddock and sow lucerne. The ostriches, their clutches of eggs now protected from predators, bred more prolifically than they had in the wild. Wing feathers could be plucked every six months or so. By 1900 some 750 000 of the birds were 'farmed', but demand continued to exceed supply and prices rose accordingly. The new wealth was reflected in a rash of ornate buildings (209) and the ostrich farmer rode high, until the vogue for feathers was blown away in the slipstream of the motor car.

◁210   211△   212▽

To the farmer of the Little Karoo both his land and the weather are animate: the earth is masculine, taciturn and reliable – though not always benevolent – while the elements are feminine, temperamental and unpredictable. It is a chauvinism of the mid-18th Century, understandable in a people whose attitudes have little changed since their forebears came to this harsh stretch of veld and koppies (**211**). Such towns as Ladismith and Oudtshoorn did enjoy a brief impetus towards progress and prosperity given by the ostrich boom. But though these towns fall within the area between the Langeberg and Swartberg ranges which geographers define as the Little Karoo, they are not truly of it.

The true Little Karoo knows no geographical limits. Rather it is a state of mind, often anachronistic in the 20th-Century world, ruggedly masculine in its individuality, often eccentric in its expression. And because it is foremost a state of mind and only secondly a region, it is appropriate that the most typical

Little Karoo town is many kilometres beyond the Swartberg mountains. Aberdeen, where Namaqualand daisies and other ephemerals blaze along the fringes of its main street (**210**), for many years boasted the highest church steeple in southern Africa. But because it was built in the spirit of the Little Karoo, the spire is glaringly unperpendicular.

In the Little Karoo money is still frequently banked in tin chests tucked under the farmer's bed. Post Offices are farmhouse kitchens where outgoing letters and parcels share the shelves with jars of preserved fruit and stamps are sold from a tea caddy. The actual mail is as often as not collected from the nearest 'dorp' or distant railway siding by donkey cart (**212**) at the convenience of the farmer/post master.

Sometimes individual idiosyncracies stand out, even in this eccentric land. Until recently a Bellair Dam farmer – one of the few in his community who had partly bowed to the trappings of the present century – drove his sheep to the market town of

213▽

215▽

214▽

Barrydale in a prewar Rolls Royce, his wife and brood of children crammed with him on the chauffeur's bench. Even in the 'Looking Glass' world of the Little Karoo eyebrows were raised – until he explained that the sliding glass window, which had once ensured privacy for stately passengers, protected his neck from the sheep's moist noses and diminished the pungent smell. In this land of pepper trees and thornbush, where in the driest regions men still move their flocks across several hundred kilometres of bare veld in search of richer pasturage (**215**), it was a simple logic which his peers could understand.

And when the rainbow's promise is made good, and she rejuvenates the land, the farmer will make his way to the church in the 'dorp' (**213**) to give thanks to a God whom he knows with utter certainty is masculine. And as the land dries out again, the presence of water again marked only by the stands of gum trees which denote each farm or wayside resting place (**214**), he will survey his taciturn fields and know life to be good.

Rising from the coastal plains of the southern Cape in a dignified splendour of golden buttresses and purple-shadowed kloofs, the Swartberg range marks an abrupt transition from rain-blessed arable lands where fields of wheat and lucerne lie rich in the sun (**216**), to the apparent poverty of the semidesert Karoo. Yet this harsh hinterland, which comprises one-third of South Africa's surface, has a richness of its own; its very aridity has led to the evolution of a unique vegetation, impressive in its variety and fascinating in its tenacity.

Broken only by flat-topped dolomite koppies or infrequently riven by grotesquely-eroded kloofs, the Karoo's brown sameness conceals a world of succulents and desert ephemerals. Euphorbias, stapelias, aloes and mesembryanthemums, whose fleshy leaves and roots allow them to store moisture, are found in an abundance of differing species. Many ephemerals, whose seeds lie dormant between the rains – sometimes several arid years apart – germinate and grow rapidly when kissed by the

218▽

first shower, and briefly carpet the veld in rainbow colours before casting their seeds to await the next moist blessing. A great number of these plants have been exported and form the nuclei of 'desert gardens' in Europe and the Americas, while Japanese plant breeders have developed the humble indigenous lithops, or stone plant, into a multihued range of vegetation more like jewels than the pebbles which the originals mimic.

There is also a rugged, albeit savage, beauty in the infrequent basalt outcrops which dot the Karoo landscape. Oases of misshapen rocks – such as the 30 and 40 m-high pinnacles of the Valley of Desolation (**217**) – break the monotony of the landscape as if to emphasize its inhospitality. In recent years the Karoo has become a very popular retreat where city dwellers, tired of hectic urban life, can be rejuvenated by the peace and tranquility of this region. Yet even in such isolated spots, man's flock find food, and the strumming of a *veewagter's* home-made guitar (**218**) is sometimes heard.

The sense of desolation of much of Africa's hinterland is echoed on the stretch of coast that points to the continent's southernmost tip and the Agulhas lighthouse which is its final punctuation (**221**). Long centuries before the white man came, clans of *Strandlopers*, Stone Age beachcombers, grubbed a meagre existence along this shore, living on shellfish and other marine life. Their presence is attested to by shell middens – their kitchen rubbish dumps – from which the modern archaeologist can piece together details of the daily life of these early inhabitants. Tidal fish-traps which the *Strandlopers*

221△   222▽

constructed are still used today not far from the coastal village of Waenhuiskrans where the quiet of picturesque fishermen's cottages, with their reed-thatched roofs (**219**), belies the rigorous existence of the occupants.

The sea here is never completely at ease. Swift tides and treacherous currents make the fisherman's life a hard one, and the waters of this coast have taken their tribute of many lives. It was near Waenhuiskrans – so named for the enormous sea-cave, accessible only at low tide (**222**), which early farmers likened to a giant coach-house – that the East Indiaman *Arniston* was wrecked in 1815 with the loss of 372 lives. And it was as Arniston, in the 1930s, that an enterprising property agent promoted the sale of beachfront cottages. But it is as Waenhuiskrans that its fisherfolk still know it, their working presence as much a reminder as the old harbour at nearby Hermanus (**220**) that most Cape coastal resorts had their beginnings in the harvest of the seas.

To early mariners, who had to struggle against the winds and currents to pass its threatening rocks, it was the 'Cape of Storms'. And while Sir Francis Drake, on his epic of circumnavigation wrote of it as 'the most stately thing, and the fairest Cape we saw in the whole circumference of the earth', the southern tip of the Cape Peninsula creates an awesome pattern of wave-wracked sea (223). Its turbulent waters are reputedly the meeting-place of the warm Agulhas Current and the icy cold Benguela in a clash of temperature that on windless days can create sudden dense fog that blankets the upper sections of the 250 m sandstone cliffs of Cape Point, yet leaves the lower-lying Cape of Good Hope (**225**) uncovered.

In 1911, the ill-fated liner *Lusitania* was wrecked off Cape Point when the lonely warning-beacon was hidden by such a fog covering the summit of Vasco da Gama Peak – then the site of the lighthouse. The disaster led to the present lighthouse being built lower down the point – probably a boon to the men who attend it, for the peak above is recognized as the windiest spot in South Africa, not only in terms of wind frequency but in its velocity as well.

And when the gales blow here, howling across the rocky outcrops and *fynbos*

225△   226▽

scrubland of the Cape of Good Hope Nature Reserve, one can sense the forces (**224**) which created the legend of the Flying Dutchman. It was to round this Cape that Van der Decken, unable to make headway against the rage of a south-easterly storm, defied the Almighty

to stop him doing so – only to find himself and his ship condemned to roam the sea forever, day and night, 'until the trump of God shall rend the sky'.

Two centuries before Van der Decken is supposed to have left Holland with his swashbuckling crew en route to Batavia in search of a fortune, the Portuguese navigator Bartolomeu Dias was spared a similar elemental battle when his small flotilla was blown hundreds of kilometres off course and became the first to round the Cape, without seeing it or realizing that they had done so. He rectified this on his return voyage and landed at Cape Maclear to erect a cross or padrão, a replica of which stands there today (**226**).

227△ 228▽ 229▽

Though more than 30 years separated their activities, a down-to-earth German and a *joie de vivre* Frenchman – one with an eye to the commercial possibilities of dried salt fish, the other with a gourmet's appreciation of rock lobster – effectively fathered South Africa's fishing industry and, in so doing, changed the face of Hout Bay.

Fish had been caught for local consumption from the first days of white settlement – and by the indigenous peoples for many hundreds of years before that. But it was not until 1867 that an immigrant farmer in the Hout Bay valley, Jacob Trautmann, decided that the shoals of snoek which teem off the Peninsula's Atlantic coastline in autumn and early winter could be harvested, salted and dried. It was a process which his Baltic ancestors had perfected generations previously. The snoek – a large mackerel-like fish with a powerful predatory jaw – tends to deteriorate more quickly than the European species with which Trautmann was familiar. However, he

devised a way of preserving it, and he found a ready market for his product among the protein-hungry workers of the sugar plantations of Mauritius. An export industry, which a century later was to see South Africa in the 'Top Ten' of the world's fishing nations, was born.

Snoek are still landed and processed at Hout Bay, although smoking has replaced Trautmann's methods to create a favoured delicacy from this fish rather than a labourer's diet. Today Hout Bay's fishing fleet (**227**) harvests other food from the sea as well. An even greater delicacy today is rock lobster. Some still remember when this too was part of the working man's daily fare and a large bag of the succulent claws and legs could be bought for a penny.

Here it was the gourmet Frenchman Lucien Plessis who realized the potential. In 1903 he bought the hull of a British barque, the *R. Morrow*, which had been wrecked off Mouille Point. He had it towed to Hout Bay and turned it into a

230▽

231▽

canning factory to process rock lobster which he exported to France. A mysterious explosion in 1914 tore the factory apart, killing M. Plessis and seven of his employees. But the fish-canning industry which he began still flourishes, and rock lobster tails processed at Hout Bay are exported to almost every segment of the globe.

The international fishing boom of the postwar years gave the fishing harbour (**228**) a fillip. Substantial accommodation for the fishermen (**229**) and their families was built as the dockside factory and processing plants expanded – much to the annoyance of the beachfront residents and inhabitants of the largely-rural valley extending beyond the dunes. It is a controversy which erupts sporadically as conservationists and industry continue an irreconcilable verbal battle.

Conservation was also far from the thoughts of the first white settlers to visit the valley. Within a month of Van Riebeeck's arrival in April 1652, his men had discovered that the valley contained many fine tall trees. A rough road was hastily built over Constantia Nek and timber was felled. Even then the needs of progress were the first to be served. In fact, the only recorded visitors to Hout Bay who left it virtually untouched appear to have been the crew of the *H.M.S. Consent*. They paused here in 1607 after sailing under the looming cliffs of Hangberg and the Sentinel to the anchorage, today guarded by a mediocre sculpture of a bronze leopard (**231**). They came briefly ashore – the Mate John Chapman was accidentally almost left behind – and then sailed on, the only sign of their visit, the words 'Chapman's Chance' marked on a chart. Today the lucky sailor is remembered in the name given to Chapman's Peak and its scenic drive (**230**) which rivals the Mediterranean Corniche for spectacle. In places sliced out of vertical rock, the road curves and winds along a breathtaking route from Hout Bay to the unbroken sweep of Noordhoek's unspoilt beach where small-boat fishermen put out to catch rock lobster.

232△   233▽   234▽   235▽

When the first colonists arrived in Table Bay to establish a provision station, they came to a land already rich in flora. It took them some time, however, to realize the wealth of edible plants awaiting them and they paid scant, if any, attention to the even greater treasure house of unique vegetation which the land encompassed. And it was a botanical treasure house; South Africa's floral kingdom is the richest in the world, with more than 18 500 indigenous flowering species alone. The *fynbos* of the Table Mountain range, in whose shadow Van Riebeeck and his tiny garrison had settled, comprises more than 2 500 forms of plant – the greatest range in Nature found so compactly.

But the settlers, whose first attempts at cultivation had failed, were more concerned with food than flora, with bread than botany. They were forced to experiment with *veldkos* – roots, herbs and the fruits of indigenous plants such as oxalis, or sorrel, and the young shoots of palmiet to provide 'greens' for their diet. This was the limit of their interest. Faced as they were with carving out a new land, their preoccupation with the utilitarian is understandable.

Yet all around them grew some of the world's most intriguing flora including the cycads (**232**), unchanged representatives of plants which flourished between 200 and 300 million years ago,

6△   237▽   238▽   239▽

before any flowering species inhabited the earth. Two genera – *Stangeria* and *Encephalartos* – are found only in South Africa. Full realization of the extent of the Cape's botanical wealth did not come about for nearly 100 years. Then, with the arrival of such skilled scientists as Masson and Thunberg, the riches were disclosed to an astonished and fascinated Europe whose botanical gardens were innundated with specimens and seeds.

There, courtier-botanists vied with each to grow such 'exotics' as the protea, with the bearded protea (**233**), pincushions (**238**) and *suikerbos*, South Africa's best-loved species (**236**), proving particularly popular.

The seeds of the common erythrina (**235**), which are a deep red with a black spot in the centre, soon became as popular as 'lucky beads' in Europe as they were among South Africa's indigenous peoples, while the sometimes grotesque flowerheads of other members of the protea family (**234**) so closely resembled those found in Australia that botanists were baffled. Only many years later did the theory of Gondwanaland and a vast continental split provide a plausible explanation. Today many of the 'exotics' are grown throughout the world and a strelitzia (**237**) is as likely to be found in Stockholm as an everlasting (**239**) in Edgebaston.

Even the aggressive facade of concrete high-rise buildings and the serpentine curves of pillar-borne freeways cannot hide the charm of Cape Town. South Africa's second largest and mother city enjoys perhaps the loveliest setting of any metropolis in the world, even though high-rise development now covers the gently sloping shore where Jan van Riebeeck and his small party landed in April 1652, to establish a victualling station for Dutch East India Company ships en route to the spice islands of the Orient. A labyrinth of offices rises on land reclaimed from the sea where his flagship, the *Drommedaris*, rode at anchor; and an enormous container terminal stretches from the beach where an earlier mariner, Antonio de Saldanha, landed in 1501.

To Saldanha is attributed the honour of being the first white person to climb Table Mountain (**240**), whose eroded sandstone grandeur dominates the city – a grandeur heightened at night during the summer months when its precipitous northern face is floodlit (**244**). The lower slopes are now denuded of the woody thickets through which the first European colonists had to force their way. The majority of the trees that grace the area today are in plantations of imported pines and eucalyptus.

The changes, begun by Van Riebeeck, have been gradual. His brief from the *Here XVII* – the Council of Seventeen in Holland – was a practical one. He was to establish a fort and a company garden, to accrue livestock from the indigenous Khoikhoi to supply the Company's

242△   243▽

244▽

passing ships with sufficient meat to make sure the crews were content and to provide enough fresh vegetables to keep them free of scurvy.

Initially, barter with the Khoikhoi proved easy, but Van Riebeeck's first attempts at cultivation were anything but successful. Winds not only leached the topsoil, but blew seeds and seedlings away. The few straggly vegetables and corn which survived this onslaught were scorched by sun and salt-laden air. Nevertheless the Company gardener, Hendrick Hendricx Boom, managed to salvage enough seed from the battered crops to ensure a second planting. This time the settlers were more successful.

Fruit trees from St Helena were cultivated and, as more land came under the plough, vines were imported from Europe. Both these introductions were to prove the first steps in developing South Africa's agricultural economy.

But if the cultivation of crops was beginning to thrive, the cultivation of good-neighbourliness with the indigenous population was not. Skirmishes with the Khoikhoi – who had grazed and hunted the lands where Cape Town's suburbs now sprawl (241) – grew increasingly frequent. A chain of forts, ancillary to the 'castle', were thrown up along the Liesbeeck River – then reed-fringed and the habitat of hippo, but today a concrete-sided canal.

Now rivalling Table Mountain as the city's premier tourist attraction is the Victoria and Alfred Waterfront (242 and 243), a converted section of Cape Town's historic working harbour which is characterized by a lively mélange of dockside entertainment.

◁245 247△ 248▽

246▽

Today tall blocks of beachfront flats resist the winds which wreaked havoc on Hendrick Boom's first attempts at cultivation, for it was at Sea Point, under the slopes of Signal Hill, that he sowed his ill-fated fields of corn. To the seafront lawn and the immense sea-water pool (245) that are features of this cosmopolitan suburb, the youth of Cape Town flock day in and day out. In high summer it becomes a mecca for a myriad holiday-makers, its restaurant-filled main street thronging with hungry visitors. But even here there is something of the *grande dame*, for the pleasures of Sea Point seem more sedate than those of Durban's frenetic Golden Mile.

249▽   250▷

And, despite the modern glass and glitter of the Foreshore, where Jan van Riebeeck's statue peers towards the mountain through the spray of playing fountains (**246**), the Mother City is sedate. In the eyes of Capetonians her serenity confirms that 'everything is for the best in this best of all possible worlds'. Strolling down Government Avenue of oaks, where Boom eventually established his vegetable garden, and past the mellow buildings which house the Republic's parliament (**247**), the visitor may forgive the dowager such smugness. She retains a dignity suited to a life that has seen the tiny first settlement grow from sod and timber to stones and bricks

and mortar. She has experienced the changes from the days of Company control, through colonial administration to self-government; and for part of each year she is the home of the country's politicians when parliament meets.

Cape Town's buildings, as much as her air of history, contribute to the proud stateliness which mantles much of the city's centre. Though sleek cars swish across the cobbles of Greenmarket Square in front of its Old Town House (**248**), the clop of horses and a trundling carriage passing these steps seems more appropriate. The Victorian splendour of the city hall, recently renovated, presides over the flower-sellers on the Grand

Parade (**250**), yet even here the idiosyncracies of the dowager are apparent. The clock in its central tower is as punctual as the noonday gun, still fired each day from the battery on the slopes of Signal Hill.

The Grand Parade has seen almost as much of the city's history as has the mountain. Now separated from the sea by railway marshalling yards and a plethora of roads and buildings, it was once part of the great bay's shoreline and was scoured by the cleansing south-east winds – the Cape Doctor. In winter the 'Doctor' rests and a blanket of fog (**249**) often lies over the Cape Flats which link the Peninsula with the rest of Africa.

Cape Town, today's serenely-poised dowager, was once a seaman's moll. Although the settlement on the shores of Table Bay had its origins as a garden, it was as a port that it reached maturity and earned the name 'Tavern of the Seas'. The bay was actually ideally suited for summer anchorage and was used regularly by passing ships after De Saldanha's discovery. But even during the summer months the sea could throw up a sudden vicious storm such as that experienced in 1647, when the Dutch *Nieuwe Haerlem* foundered on a sandbank near present-day Milnerton. Some of the *Nieuwe Haerlem's* crew spent more than a year ashore protecting her valuable cargo.

254△   255▽

Though their temporary settlement did not influence the Council of Seventeen's decision to establish a way-station at the Cape, their experience proved valuable in planning a permanent maritime outpost.

By the time the small colony was established and the first Free Burgher farmers had begun to cultivate the land in earnest, ships of all the world's maritime nations were making use of Table Bay. In the grog shops and taverns of the waterfront Spanish reals, English pounds and French louis were as acceptable as the Dutch gulden. Table Bay was at times a forest of masts and spars and some 50 ships were anchored here when, during a severe storm in 1722, 11 British

and Dutch ships were wrecked. However, maritime activity, which continues today (**251**), reached its peak in the 1950s and 1960s when the closure of the Suez Canal returned the Cape to its role as a haven for ships of all nations.

There is no record of how long it took De Saldanha and his fellow mariners to climb what he named Taboa de Cabo or 'Table Cape', though he probably followed the steep but easy route up the Platteklip Gorge which gashes the mountain-face above the city. The aerial cableway (**252**), which began operation in 1929, whisks the modern visitor to the plateau summit in a matter of minutes. A viewing area near the upper cable station

provides a spectacular vista of the Peninsula, including the immense sweep of Table Bay (**253**) with its western bastion of Lion's Head and its Rump, now known as Signal Hill.

Where Table Mountain's summit provides superb views of the bay and the city, Rhodes Memorial (**254**) on the lower, south-eastern slopes of Devil's Peak is an equally fine vantage-point from which to view the sprawl of development creeping across the Cape Flats towards the distant Hottentots Holland mountains. Nearby is the Groote Schuur estate, Rhodes' home (**255**) which served for many years as the Prime Minister's official residence.

On its Atlantic side the rocky spine of the Cape Peninsula plunges steeply to the sea. Here the sheer face of the mountain is cut by a spectacular series of kloofs and ravines into a chain of buttresses which Van Riebeeck described as the *Gewelbergen* (or Gable Mountain). Today they are known as the Twelve Apostles (**256**) – something of a misnomer, as 18 of the outcrops guard the mountain's flank before it dips to the gentle curve of Hout Bay. Nestling at their feet are some of the Cape's most popular beaches, where – perhaps because the water is colder than that of False Bay – the youthful and the no-longer-so-youthful come to see and be seen rather than to swim. These are the bikini beaches of Clifton and Camps Bay (**257**) where the sun sets late and a tan is more important than the state of the surf or the temperature of the water.

The beaches of False Bay are arguably finer, and Kipling maintained that 'the white sands of Muizenberg' which 'marched silver to the sea' were the finest in the world. Poetic

258△   260△   261▽

licence perhaps, but there are many who would agree with him. Muizenberg, though it is often whipped by the summer's prevalent south-easterly winds, was the Peninsula's most popular resort, drawing thousands of inland holidaymakers. And though many of its hotels have closed, its 'snake pit' – where oiled bodies bask in profusion – still exerts its powerful attraction. The long sweep of Sunrise Beach with its attendant lines of bathing boxes (**259**) offers a sense of unmatched space and freedom. Here, too, a surfer finds freedom of a differnt sort as he rides the steep slope of a breaking wave as it rolls towards the beach (**258**) while a fishing boat passes unconcerned on its return to the nearby harbour of Kalk Bay. And in the lonely moments waiting for the swell to rise (**260**), he may hear the lowing of ghostly cattle, for Muizenberg had its origins in 1673 as a humble cattle post whose herdsman's house – recently restored – is said to be second only to the Castle as the Republic's oldest extant building.

Muizenberg was transformed in status to an important military outpost when Simon's Bay became the official winter anchorage of the Dutch East India Company's fleet. In 1795 it echoed to the sound of cannon and musket-fire when troops landed here and defeated the Dutch garrison in what proved to be the decisive battle leading to the first British occupation of the Cape and the end of the Company's control.

At nearby Fish Hoek (**261**) a battle of a different sort continues to this day, as proponents and opponents of an historic ban on liquor argue whether or not the town should remain 'dry' – the only teetotal municipality in South Africa. The ban dates from 1818 when Lord Charles Somerset granted the 1 117 ha on which the town stands to a farmer, Andries Bruins, on condition that the right to fish should remain free and that no public wine-house should be opened. Along the beach fishermen still ply their trek-nets without hinderance, and a plethora of clubs testify to Fish Hoek's 'aridity'.

262△   263▽

Lord Charles Somerset's gubernatorial ban on wine sales extended no further than Fish Hoek, but there may well have been times when he wished that it did. When he took office in 1814 the flourishing wine industry was in disarray, the once-high reputation of Cape wines had fallen to a nadir, and attempts by his predecessor to stop the rot by appointing an official taster for export wines had failed. Lord Charles was no more successful. Cape wines continued to be exported to Britain at a rate of some three million litres a year, but they were considered suitable only for cheap blending.

The situation which the Governor inherited stemmed directly from the

264△   265 ▽   266▽

Napoleonic wars and Whitehall's decision to turn the Cape into her private wine cellar. Britain encouraged production by a series of tariff preferences which backfired when the wine farmers of the western Cape opted for quick, handsome profits at the cost of quality.

Today's Cape wines have regained their high reputation and are exported throughout the free world. Their quality has been strictly controlled by the K.W.V. whose cellars at Paarl house the world's largest maturing casks (**264**).

Soon after his arrival, Van Riebeeck urged the authorities in Holland to supply him with vines, arguing that they should be as successful on the local hillsides as they were on those of France and Spain. But it was not until three years later, in 1655, that the first vines arrived and almost four years after that, in February 1659, that he recorded: 'Today, praise be to God, the wine was made for the first time from Cape grapes ...'

The early success of these official oenological efforts encouraged the Free Burghers to follow suit. By the time that Simon van der Stel retired to his homestead Groote Constantia (**263**), in whose cellars (**262**) wine is still produced, over 400 000 vines had already been planted. But wine-making was not part of the Dutch agricultural tradition and the early wines were of poor quality. It was not until 1688 and the arrival of the French Huguenots, who brought with them wine-making expertise, that production went from strength to strength and the reputation of 'Constantia' grew.

Whether that reputation would ever have been recorded from the mediocrity of the early 19th Century but for the devastation of *Phylloxera*, is moot. When this virus attacked the local vineyards in 1886, exports of the inferior product were booming. But in a matter of months the vines were almost exterminated and the old wine-presses (**265**) fell silent. Recovery with virus-resistant stocks was slow, encouraging a return to quality in today's harvest (**266**).

Of the French Protestant refugees who fled their homeland to England and Holland following the revocation of the Edict of Nantes, a mere 200 made their way to the Cape in 1688-89. But this handful was to have a disproportionate impact on South Africa's development; not only did the Huguenots give impetus to the young wine industry, but they brought with them an invigorating culture which the Dutch and German burghers lacked. The Free Burghers, former Dutch East India Company employees who were granted land after a contractual period of service, were mainly of poor peasant stock and had little of the newcomers' refinement. At the Cape the

269△ 270▽

271▽

Huguenots were allowed their own church council and minister of religion, but they were not permitted to form a separate community. Instead they were intermingled among existing farms in the Drakenstein area and the Franschhoek valley, where a striking monument (267) commemorates their contribution to South Africa's development.

The growing wealth of the Cape farmers, to which the Huguenots' skills contributed, found visible expression in a unique form of architecture – the Cape Dutch style, characterized by soaring gables. Though these gables owed something to those of the high narrow townhouses of Holland, in the open spaces of the African landscape they evolved a grace of their own. Their uniquely fine proportions can be appreciated in the solitary splendour of a rural manor house (271) as readily as in the streets of a growing town. Those of Tulbagh (268), restored to their original glory after the town was devastated by an earthquake in the late 1960s, are a perfect example. Their interiors, typified by the furnishing in Paarl's Pastorie Museum (270), echo both the grace of this style of building and the new-found wealth of those farmers. More functional but also elegant in its simple lines is the VOC Kruithuis (269), or powder magazine, built on Stellenbosh's De Braak in 1777.

272△   275▷

273△   274▽

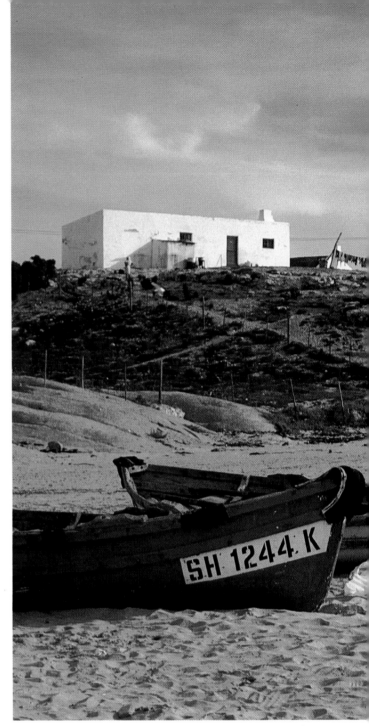

Time has marked a myriad changes in the Boland as elsewhere in South Africa, but there are pockets along the country's bleak west coast where if the clock has not stopped, it has at least slowed down. This is where the small fishing villages and hamlets follow a pattern of existence which has little changed in the past 100 years and a donkey cart (272) trundling past an old church with its attendant bell-towers is not yet an anachronism. On the fringes of the bay, small boats still line the beach above high-water (275). Their owners' reed-thatched cottages have changed no more than have their fishing methods, while at Churchhaven at the further end of the Langebaan Lagoon, where the receding tides leave the salt-flats bare (274), life-styles have deteriorated.

The three hamlets which comprise Churchhaven once boasted a thriving fishing-based community, but now they linger on only to accommodate their aged. Diminishing in-shore catches and the closure of the nearby Donkergat whaling station, formerly a source of employment for both men and women, reduced their inhabitants' livelihood to subsistence and drove the young people to seek work in the town or in the larger fishing centres of the coast. Now only the areas' popularity as a weekend retreat for the rat-race-weary inhabitants of Cape Town promises a future. Other villages face a similar fate, yet the fishermen continue their calling (**276**) despite its meagre return (**277**).

Saldanha Bay, however, has seen a recent development as the iron-ore terminal serving the inland mines at Sishen. From here almost daily, iron-ore trains – often more than a kilometre long – hurtle across the wastes of the northern Cape to discharge their cargo into the waiting holds of bulk carriers. The piers of the terminal, resting on the fossilized remains of a two-million-year-old oyster bed, provide a back-drop to the deep-sea fishing boats returning to a bustling harbour with their catches (**273**).

276▽

277▽

Across the shimmering heat haze of the Karoo a distant beacon beckons and the dust-weary traveller feels the same sense of relief that the early trekkers through this semidesert must have felt when the oxen quickened their pace at the scent of water. The beacon is a church spire, mark of every town in this landscape of desolate beauty and a welcome break in a horizon fringed only with flat-topped koppies. Nothing is visible in this arid waste to indicate that it was once an enormous, steaming swamp in which life developed over 300 million years ago. Yet in its shales the Karoo holds hidden the fossil remains of aconites – among the earliest of life forms – of fish and of mammal-like reptiles that bridged the evolutionary span between water and land. Then these parts were moist and lush; today they are semidesert.

Technically the Karoo covers one-third of South Africa and it is slowly continuing to spread eastwards. It is marked more by its vegetation than by any geographical boundaries. The plants have a high nutritional value, but are generally so sparse that some 4 hectares of veld is required to feed each of the sheep or goats (**279**) on which the Karoo's agriculture is based. Colesberg (**278**) breaks slightly with this pattern as an important horse-breeding centre. Otherwise, with Graaff-Reinet, it best typifies the centres of Karoo farming. Colesberg was established in the first half of the 19th Century on the site of an abandoned London Missionary station. Plots on the main street were sold to finance the building of the Dutch Reformed Church which dominates the town. Its early houses, many of which still stand, are a fascinating architectural combination of Cape Dutch and Georgian styles and were built with flat roofs because of the lack of suitable thatching reeds in the vicinity.

But there are man-made oases other than those marked by the beacons of church spires. Despite its arid surface drabness,

▷278　279△

280△　281▽

there is considerable underground water in the Karoo. Where man has tapped it, often boring hundreds of metres into the rocky shale to do so, the green of lawns, gardens and the ubiquitous lucerne marks a typical farmstead (**280**).

To the modern traveller, Matjiesfontein presents an oasis of a different, probably more welcome sort. This village, established as a health resort in the 1880s and today a popular hotel complex, was the first in South Africa to have water-borne sewerage. The London street lamps with which the village's founder clocked up another first – electricity – still light its only street (**281**). The turret of the Lord Milner Hotel, built during the early stages of the second Anglo-Boer War, was later used as a look-out post when the village was commandeered as the headquarters of a 12 000-strong British garrison. It was from these troops that the force intended to relieve the siege of Kimberley was drawn, only to suffer a heavy defeat at the battle of Magersfontein.

A giant crater 1 097-m-deep is today the empty reminder of the discovery in 1866 of a 'pretty pebble' that was to change the course of South African history. It was not until 1870 that the first of four diamondiferous blue-ground pipes was discovered where Kimberley now stands. The 21,75-carat diamond which 15-year-old Erasmus Jacobs found on the bank of the Orange River awakened geologists and prospectors to the presence in the north-eastern Cape of the hardest and most treasured of all known crystals.

The nine-metre-high Colesberg Koppie, which was the last of the four pipes uncovered, soon disappeared under the picks and shovels of the diggers to

282△   283▽

become the Big Hole (**282**) – the biggest hole ever dug by man without the aid of machines. Prospectors flocked from other claims, established in the two previous years, to the site. As the diggers delved ever deeper into the diamond-rich Kimberlite, pathways which had criss-crossed the claims disappeared and opencast mining developed. Small claims were bought out, but 14 years after the excavations started there were still 98 operators. It was then that Cecil Rhodes and his partners began the financial machinations which led to the creation of De Beers Consolidated Mines, the most powerful force in the world's diamond market. When mining of the

284△   285▽

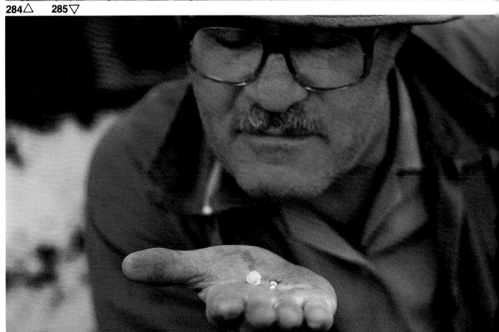

Big Hole ceased in 1914, it had yielded more than three tonnes (14 504 375 carats) of diamonds.

Kimberley remains the centre of diamond sorting (**283**) and also where the small private prospectors (**285**) bring their finds for valuation and sale.

The early mining days are also linked to 'Long Cecil', the field gun standing in the shadow of the town's war memorial (**284**). Designed and built at Rhodes' request during the siege of Kimberley, it was the creation of American mining engineer George Labram, and proved so successful that the Boers used their 'Long Tom' in retaliation – its last shot killing Labram who was resting in his hotel.

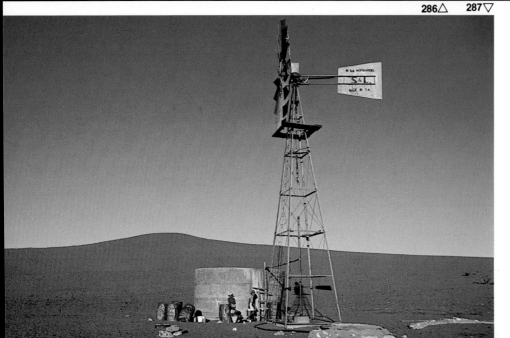

The red-brown sands of the desert seem to stretch forever, their colours mirrored by cloudscapes as the sun settles behind the horizon of the Kalahari. It is a stark landscape where the passing of a donkey with its rider is noteworthy and the passage of two is an event (286)! It is a land better suited to the gemsbok (288) than to man, a lost corner of the Northern Cape which nevertheless saw the brief fruition of not one, but two ill-fated republics – Stellaland and Goshen.

Both came into being as the result of inter-tribal warfare among the Bechuana, or Tswana, who had inhabited this empty

288△ 289▽

land for centuries before the first white explorers probed north to the fabled Kingdom of Latakoo. In 1882 the pro-British Batlapin chief Mankurwane was defeated by the Korana chief David Massouw, the latter achieving victory with the armed assistance of a group of Transvaal burghers. As a reward for their aid, Massouw granted the Transvaalers a tract of land reaching north and south of the Harts River. Here, in August 1883, they established the 'Republic of the Star', or Stellaland, with Vryburg as its capital. The newly-founded republic adopted the constitution of the neighbouring Transvaal, designed its own flag and coat of arms and even issued its own postage stamps. It seemed set to enjoy peaceful prosperity.

Moves were begun to incorporate Stellaland with the Transvaal but, before negotiations were concluded, the London Convention of 1884 fixed the western limits of the Transvaal, excluding Stellaland, so that the tiny Boer enclave was forced to remain isolated.

A similar fate befell the Republic of Goshen, which had been established a year earlier than Stellaland and some distance to the north. Its origins also lay in a clash of black tribes – in this instance Moswete of the Kunwana defeated a Barolong chief – the victor awarding a substantial grant of land to the Boers who had aided him. A 'capital' was established at a spot appropriately named Rooigrond, or 'red earth', and affiliation with the Transvaal Republic was sought. Both fledgling republics surrendered to a British invasion force in 1885, without bloodshed or even a shot being fired. Both the republics were incorporated into what was then Bechuanaland Protectorate; a decade later they joined the Cape.

Possibly the burghers – isolated and without even a viable agricultural economy – were glad to see the last of the two short-lived states. Certainly the land remains little loved, its silence disturbed only by the clack of an infrequent windmill (287) or the bleating of a flock of goats (289).

290△ 291▽

Sun City, where the fun never stops, is set in the dun and green grasslands two hours' drive to the north of Johannesburg and Pretoria. It is southern Africa's answer to Las Vegas: a glittering and unashamedly hedonistic fun factory whose four hotels and crowded gaming rooms are designed to distract, amuse and pamper three million visitors a year. Outdoor relaxation features prominently in the scheme. Among the several sparkling swimming pools is one that embraces an island of tall Washingtonia and phoenix date palms (**290**); other even more spectacular venues are Waterworld,

292 △

293 △   294 ▽

a 750-metre man-made lushly-fringed lake, and the Water-scape, a sequence of three interlinked pools, 12 waterfalls and 2 km of walkways that take you through some of the most exquisite of landscaped grounds.

The focus of indoor activity is the Entertainment Centre, a busy concentration of restaurants, bars, discos, cinemas, acres of slot machines (**293**), the exuberant Extravaganza Theatre (**294**), the famed casino and the 7 000-seat Superbowl, used for conventions, international title-fights and for the annual Miss World contest.

The pride of Sun City, though, is the Lost City development, central feature of which is the Palace of the Lost City (**291** and **292**), an overwhelming construction of domes and minarets, ultra-luxurious suites, an entrance hall that rises three storeys and, in the grounds, an instant 'jungle' of beautiful trees and a sparkling 100-by-60-metre swimming pool which is swept by artificially-created surfing waves.